SATIRES

Carlos Whitlock Porter

Cartoons by A. Wyatt Mann

SATIRES
By Carlos Whitlock Porter

(c) 2013 by Carlos Whitlock Porter. All rights reserved.

http://www.cwporter.com

Cartoons by A. Wyatt Mann.
Used by permission of Tom Metzger,
P.O. Box 401 Warsaw, Indiana 46581
tm_metzger@yahoo.com

*Dedicated to
A. Wyatt Mann, one of the greatest comic artists
since John Tenniel: a man of infinite wit,
inexhaustible ideas, unflinching courage,
and a muse of fire.*

Warning: Contains racially explicit material. For adults only.

Table of Contents

Introduction 7

A Manifesto 9

A Dilemma 13

An Apology 17

Is Race Really Just Skin Deep? 18

Jud Süss – Coming Soon to an Economy Near You 21

On AIDS 22

On the Banking System 39

On Christianity 44

On Debt 48

On Democracy 52

On Globalization 63

On Immigration 66

On Multiculturalism 72

On Slavery 77

On Stalin 83

On the Gulf War 87

Pseudozoological Satire #1 90

Pseudozoological Satire #2 91

Reply to an English Anti-Anti-Semite 97

Standard "Hate" Accusation Reply Form 100

The Aristotelian Connection 113

The Free Market 123

The Master Plan 125

Upon Being Convicted of "Incitement to Racial Hatred" 128

In Memoriam – A Dedication 132

INTRODUCTION

Many years ago, someone I know very well worked as a trained children's nurse in a world-famous hospital for disturbed children, in London, with 4 years of training (RN, RSCN) and about 8 years of experience. All the other staff members were similarly qualified. The head of the unit was, obviously, a qualified physician, with 20 years of experience working with disturbed children.

One day two Jews showed up, both of them 22 years old, one from South Africa, the other from Canada, neither one of them with any medical training or experience, but with 4-year "psychology degrees".

They created total chaos throughout the entire hospital, from the day they arrived, until the day they left.

They said that the children should be allowed to "express themselves" by refusing to do what they were told, by hitting and kicking members of staff, by spitting on members of staff, etc. etc.

If you didn't agree with what they said, you were accused of "not wanting to be progressive", etc. etc.

They would argue the hind leg off a mule, and were adept at "proving" that $2 + 2 = 6$.

The English being what they are – wishy-washy – in short order these two Jews had everybody fighting and quarrelling with everybody else.

The doctor in charge of the unit simply opted out.

In the end, after several months, they both left, presumably to wreak havoc elsewhere, and things returned more or less to normal.

This is how the Jews *always* operate, at all times and in all places: they get *everybody* fighting with each other, over crazy theories invented by *them*, and it only stops when *they* leave or are expelled.

This has been the history of the Jews for 3,000 years, wherever they have ever lived, from the distant past to the present.

That repression causes neurosis is a truism of the modern world, a notion invented and peddled chiefly by Jews and originally, but not exclusively, by the Freudians. Good manners, discretion, a decent sense of shame, a consideration for the feelings and sensitivity of others are a thing of the past. This applies chiefly to sexual matters.

This does not apply, of course, to the "repression" of our natural resentment of buttinsky yidniks and other by-products of the primeval ooze. What about *our* self-expression? What about *our* mental health? We should bust a gut or something? We might become neurotic, already?

It is the hypothesis of this practitioner (i.e., myself) that millions of white Americans are suffering from neurotic symptoms caused by the repression of their racial feelings. Freud believed that neurosis would cure itself through the "catharsis" [κάθαρσις] of analysis, i.e., the "expression" [*Äußerung*] of "repressed feelings" [*verdrängten Empfindungen*].

Hence the present volume.

Carlos Whitlock Porter,
16 September 2013

A MANIFESTO

Environmental Cleansing

No matter where we look, the world faces seemingly insoluble problems. In fact, these problems are not insoluble at all, as we shall soon see.

We are told that the white man's way of life is incompatible with the future of the planet, and simultaneously that we must create 800 million jobs in the Third World to give the undeveloped countries a modern standard of living.

Of course, if the first part of the proposition is correct, our way of life must be restricted as much as possible (i.e., to whites only), and there is no need for 800 million jobs.

We are told that the Brazilians are cutting down irreplaceable rainforests because of poverty and overpopulation to engage in industrial processes which have been obsolete in Europe for centuries (such as steel manufacture using charcoal for fuel). When told that they are endangering the world's oxygen supply, their reply (translated from their Brazilian nigger talk) is, "Man, we ain't gonna be de ga'bage can fo' cleanin' up yo' dirty air".

[Note: Actually, what happened is that Brazil, like many countries, accepted foreign aid from Britain and the USA to "modernise their steel industry" while protecting their own products with high tariffs, as a result of which their steel industry is now ultra-modern, and we have none left. This was said to demonstrate "the efficiency of the free market".]

Well, in that case, we must simply cut down on pollution (fewer factories producing useless junk to be sold to Brazilians on money that we loan them). We must also cut down on Brazilians (average I.Q. of "street children" according to National Geographic: 55).

Fortunately, the Brazilians are doing their bit to kill themselves off with train surfing, elevator surfing, drug wars, and glue sniffing. Who says there's no order in the universe?

We are told that we owe reparations for slavery. The problem here is, who gets the money? American niggers say Africans should get nothing because they sold their brothers into slavery, while Africans say American niggers should get nothing because they have benefited by living in America.

No problem there. Africans get nothing because they sold their brothers into slavery, while American niggers get nothing because they have benefited from living in America.

We are told that we are the cause of all the niggers' problems. Of course, if that is so, the niggers are better off without us, and don't need our help. No problem there.

We are told that we gassed the Jews, exterminated the Indians, and enslaved the niggers, and that we are a race of criminals.

Of course, if that is so, it would be absurd for us to feel guilty. I never met a criminal yet who felt guilty for anything, have you? On the contrary, we should reflect that there are criminal enterprises open to us which we have not even exploited yet.

We are told that America must be run for the benefit of non-whites on the grounds of "Minority Rights", while South Africa must be run for the benefit of non-whites on the grounds of "Majority Rule".

No problem there. America should be run for the benefit of whites on the grounds of "Majority Rule", while South Africa should be run for the benefit of whites on the grounds of "Minority Rights" (white rights).

We are told of a wave of criminal violence in Germany in which five Turks were recently burnt to death. No problem there. If the niggers in South Africa can burn each other's heads off with nothing but applause from the world's liberals, surely the Germans, in the interest of fairness, must be allowed to toast a Turk from time to time. Why not? Anything else would be a double standard, which is repugnant to our sense of justice.

Since nobody sees a need to protect whites in South Africa, surely there is no need to protect Turks in Germany.

We are told that homosexuals and lesbians are "born that way" and "just can't help it", and, simultaneously, that we must allow them to turn the public school system, Boy and Girl Scouts, children's television, etc. etc. into vehicles of "gay" propaganda, filling 5-year-olds with guilt and shame for whatever heterosexual tendencies they may be fortunate enough to possess, arresting third-graders for kissing girls on the playground, etc. etc., *ad infinitum et ad nauseam*, thus breeding a nation of bull dykes and faggots: the world's first homosexual totalitarian dictatorship.

Of course, if the first part of the proposition is correct, then there is no need for any indoctrination and propaganda. No problem there.

We are told that we must practise birth control and murder one and one-half million of our own unborn children per year through abortion because "There Are Too Many People in the World", and simultaneously that we need 70 million African immigrants in Europe over the next 20 years "To Create Economic Growth" and "To Pay the Pensions of an Ageing Population".

No problem there. 70 million African immigrants "swim with the fish" because "There Are Too Many People in the World", then we quadruple our birth rate in Europe (the white birth rate) "To Create Economic Growth" and "To Pay the Pensions of an Ageing Population". The only thing we have to worry about now is "Mad Tuna Disease".

The nigger is a spiritual animal and can't feel a thing from the waist up. It's a proven fact. He doesn't mind if you burn his head off with a mixture of Diesel fuel and melting rubber, but he suffers unspeakable agonies of soul at the sight of a "Whites Only" sign on a park bench. How pitiless! How cruel! (or so the liberals tell us).

By some coincidence, I have a similar theory regarding the liberals which I intend to test at the earliest possible opportunity.

Since I don't like to cause pain, I shall be most upset if this theory proves incorrect. I therefore propose the following experiment: We necklace a nigger radical (Nelson Mandela) simultaneously with a white traitor (De Klerck or Helmut Kohl) to test the pain threshold of different races. This would allow scientific knowledge to be gained despite the possible falsity of the original hypothesis.

1994–2001

A DILEMMA

I don't suppose it occurs to people that the Jews are placing the world upon the horns of a dilemma.

Let's be logical. Either Hitler gassed the Jews, or he didn't.

Let's say he did.

He Gassed Them

The Jews say the Germans killed 2/3 of the Jews in Europe. If that is true, it means that American intervention in Europe – which cost us (the Americans) a trillion dollars and 250,000 lives – saved 1/3 of the Jews in Europe from certain destruction.

I repeat: If Hitler gassed 2/3, then we saved 1/3. The Jews can't have it any other way.

That being the case, do we get any gratitude? Of course not. Instead, all of the accusations that used to be made against the Germans are now made against the White Race as a whole.

The Pope is guilty for the Holocaust (or so the Jews say).

Christianity is guilty for the Holocaust (or so the Jews say).

Western civilization is guilty for the Holocaust (or so the Jews say).

We are all guilty for the Holocaust (or so the Jews say).

Maybe some day life will be discovered on other planets, so that we can hear about how Martians and Venusians are guilty for the Holocaust.

Our guilt for the Holocaust can never be erased (or so the Jews say).

Centuries, eons, ages, may pass, but our guilt for the Holocaust will remain (or so the Jews say).

When our culture, nation, and race have become extinct through immigration, abortion, race-mixing, the constant promotion of homosexuality and Zero Birth Rate as a way of life, etc. etc., our guilt for the Holocaust will remain, unextinguished for all time (or so the Jews say).

When all the industry is in China and all the Chinese are in Europe; when car-theft, drug-pushing, and whoring are the only gainful occupations left; when our sons have all become AIDS-infected drug addicts or drag queens; when our daughters have all become race-mixing, guilt-obsessed field sluts, aborting their own children and adopting Africans instead, our guilt for the Holocaust will remain, unextinguished for all time (or so the Jews say).

No country lives in the past. No country spends all its time worrying about something that happened in a foreign country fifty years ago. Whatever Hitler did to the Jews, it was a matter between foreigners. It's not only something other nations had nothing to do with, it's something we put a stop to, at considerable cost to ourselves.

Hundreds of millions of people have been killed in the twentieth century (usually because the Jews wanted it that way), but no matter; only Jews are important.

Only Jews have rights; only Jews have feelings. I have four children educated in Catholic schools. They know nothing about the Christian religion. They know nothing about the Bible. They know nothing about the Middle Ages or the Renaissance. They've never heard of Communism or Stalin. But they know all about Auschwitz. They know all about homosexuals, transsexuals, transvestites, condoms and AIDS, because they learn it in school!

They never once visited Waterloo, one of the world's most famous battlefields, located right outside Brussels; or "Flanders' Fields", where millions died; they never visited Ghent; or Antwerp; or Brugge (Bruges), the "Venice of the North", with some of the most beautiful public buildings, museums, cathedrals and art treasures in all of Europe; but they saw "Swindler's Mist" with the *whole school* and visited Auschwitz *twice*.

I sent four children to Catholic schools and all the priests were ever interested in was the promotion of miscegenation. Provided you flood Europe with Africans or brain-damaged Asians in wheelchairs, you can have as many abortions as you like, and do anything you want sexually. I remedied many of the deficiencies in their education myself, simply by spending time with them and talking to them whenever they were interested in something.

This is all that is left of the religion that produced thousands of martyrs and built the cathedrals of Europe.

This is the world that tens of millions of people died for.

The Jews say they want a G-d world. But what they have given us is a filth world, an excrement world; in short, a J-w world.

It used to be that the Jews only wished to destroy the Germans. That day is finished. Now they want to destroy us all.

All law, all morals, all art, all culture, all religion must be perverted and destroyed to suit the Jews. Why?

Because of the Holocaust. Because a foreigner killed foreign

Jews.

I have faith in my children. They are good children. But I see no future for them. They remind me of goldfish swimming in a sewer.

They seem to think it perfectly natural that their future should be blotted out for the benefit of billions of Africans and Asians; that the world should be filled with disease to avoid interfering with the pleasures of deviants; that there should be no future for white children.

If you have four children and they are white, people treat you like a sex-fiend, like you can't control yourself. So many children!!!

But all the other races can have eight or ten, and that is wonderful. We are supposed to feed them, care for them, cure their diseases, admit them as immigrants, provide them with a modern standard of living; we must LITERALLY prefer them over our own children!

And what is the excuse for it all? Because a foreigner killed foreign Jews!

No matter where in the world we live, we can't write our own immigration laws without interference from the Jews. We can't even expel illegal immigrants without interference from the Jews, because it reminds them of "when they were being rounded up for the Holocaust", etc. etc.

The cave paintings at Lescaux and Altamira are among the most beautiful artistic creations in history, and they are 20,000 years old. Yet the race that created them is doomed to extinction.

What is our guilt? Is it some crime we committed? No. We are being destroyed for an act of kindness. We took pity on the Jews.

This means that we are doomed to become extinct as a race because of something some foreigner did to a load of foreigners 50 years ago!

So what is the lesson to be learned from all this? That the Jews are ungrateful?

Of course not. Jewish ingratitude has been proverbial since Biblical times.

Every act of kindness shown to them becomes a new injustice to be expiated through eternal atonement (and hundreds of tons of gold).

No. The real lesson of the Holocaust (assuming that it is an historical fact) is that, with Jews, partial killing and pogroms DO NOT WORK.

If you could kill 90% of them, it would teach the remaining 10% absolutely NOTHING. They would NEVER understand that they had it coming to them TO ANY EXTENT AT ALL, even 1%.

The lesson of the Holocaust is that partial killing of Jews does not work – it must be ALL or NOTHING. Really, we should thank the Jews for making matters so clear to us.

Since killing all the Jews is impossible and should not be attempted, but since the Jews never seem to learn anything and since Israel is a failure, perhaps the Jews will be kind enough to colonize the moon to escape anti-Semitism?

Perhaps it could be paid for out of reparations collected from the Palestinians.

Now let's look at the other horn of the dilemma.

He Gassed Them Not

Of course, the above only applies if the Holocaust is a "proven fact", i.e., if Hitler really gassed the Jews.

If it's all lies – and a filthy, disgusting, degrading pack of lies at that, then the situation is incomparably worse.

1998

UNCLE SHAM WANTS YOURS

IT APPEARS THAT THE STARS OF DAVID AND STRIPES OF AUSCHWITZ WILL BE WITH US FOREVER

AN APOLOGY

HOW DO LIKE THIS? A SCUMBAG HOLLYWOOD ACTOR FINALLY HAS THE BALLS TO SPEAK CANDIDLY ABOUT THE KIKES AND WHAT HAPPENS?

I see by the papers that Marlon Brando has apologized to the JEWS for referring to them as "KIKES". I feel that this gesture shows great magnanimity of character, and deserves to be widely emulated. Since "KIKE" is a noun, only, however, while "JEW" is both a verb and noun, and since both words mean the same thing, it therefore follows that the word "JEW" is at least twice as offensive as the word "KIKE".

I therefore apologize to the KIKES of the world for referring to them as JEWS. I deeply regret all the pain and suffering which I may inadvertently have inflicted upon this ancient race of coprophiliacs, urolagniacs, menstruophobes, incest addicts, child rapists, child murderers, slavers, pimps, pornographers, con artists, genocide artists, bloodsuckers, extortioners, and purveryors of filth generally, by the crude, offensive, and vulgar term of abuse – JEW – rather than by the proper term of respect, which is – KIKE.

I trust that the present apology will be accepted in the spirit in which it is intended.

1992

IS RACE REALLY JUST SKIN DEEP

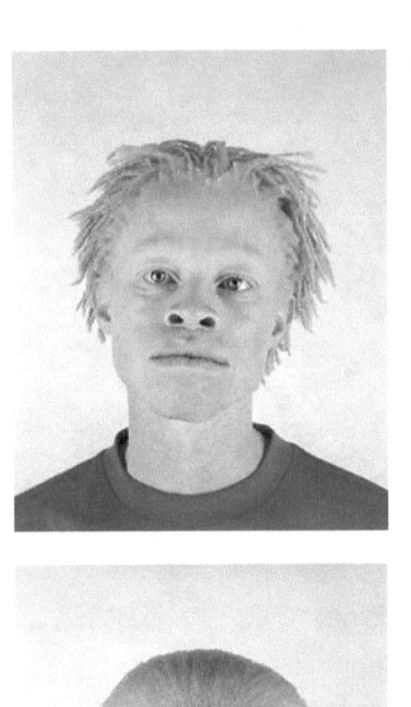

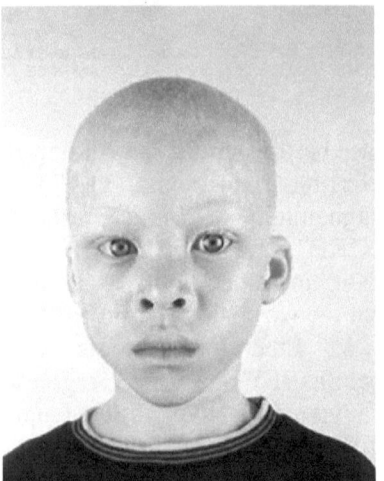

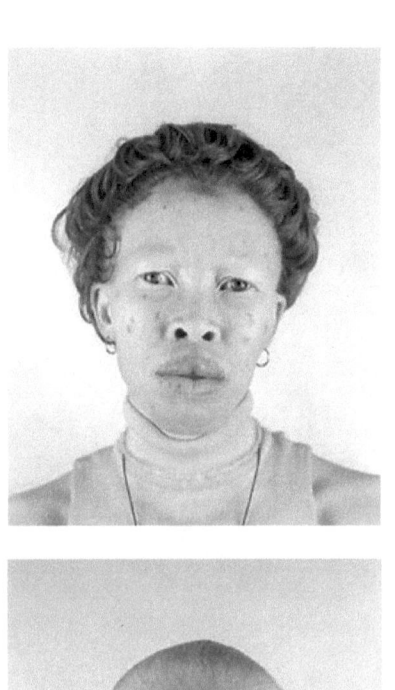
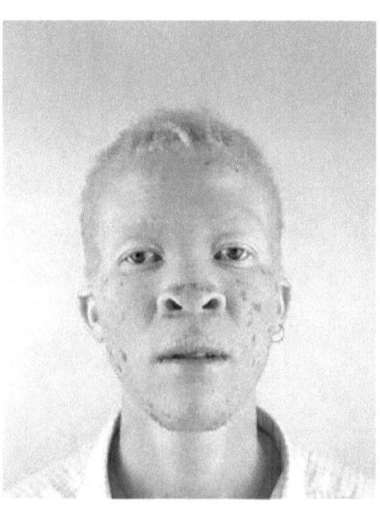
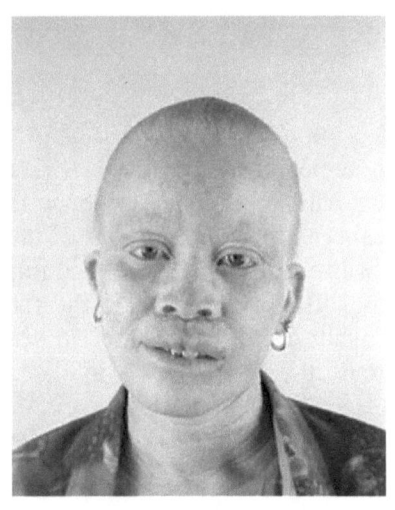
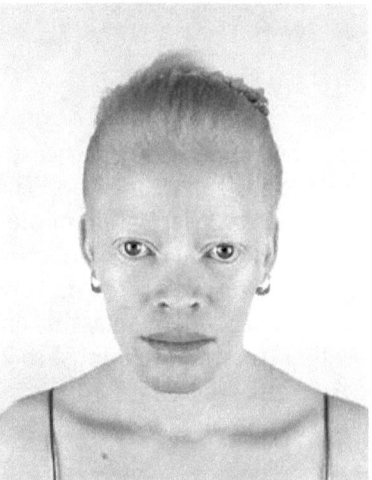

 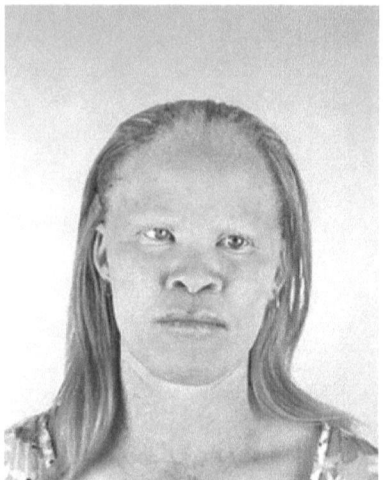

Well, now, apparently not, because these people are obviously Africans – full-blooded Africans, too. They are African albinos – a not-so-rare genetic defect. Most of them die of cancer. There are millions of these people. Yet their "skin colour" is as white as yours (I hope) and mine. Anybody who claims to perceive "no difference" between the races needs glasses – dark glasses, and a white cane. Is it "hate" to see a speeding truck before it crushes you to death?

2007

JUD SÜSS – COMING SOON TO AN ECONOMY NEAR YOU

In the famous 1940 National Socialist film, the Jew Joseph Süss Oppenheimer ("Jud Süss") loans the Duke of Württemburg so much money that it can never possibly be repaid, so, in return, Jews are allowed to flood the Dukedom and privatize all the infrastructure (roads, bridges, etc.).

Everything is paid for many times over, with toll booths every few miles on every road, etc., ruining the economy of the Dukedom and leading to eventual revolution.

Sound familiar?

Ferdinand Marian as "Jud Süss".
Coming soon to an economy near you.

ON AIDS

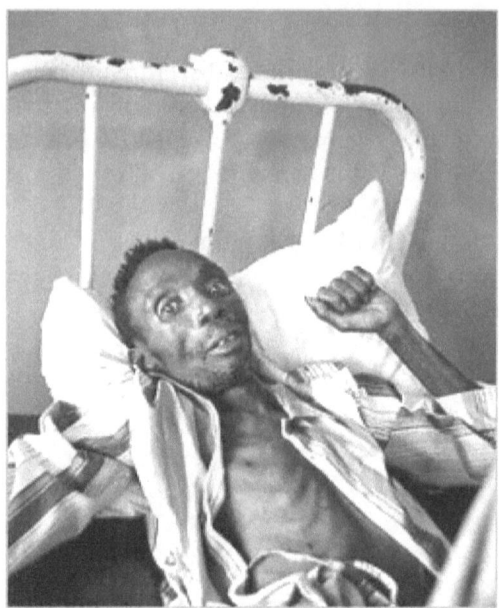

In the 19th century, an English merchant contracted to deliver one grain of wheat, the number of grains to double every day until the contract expired. He then discovered that he had contracted to deliver more wheat than existed anywhere in the world; more, in fact, than all the world's grain supplies put together. The contract was declared null and void.

This little swindle was based on a curious phenomenon of mathematics called "Exponential Doubling". It works this way: if you take the number 1 and double it 10 times, it comes to more than a thousand. Double it 20 times, and it comes to more than a million. Double it 30 times, it comes to more than a billion.

Let us take two other examples:

a) If there are 1 billion non-whites in the world (using the figure 1 to simplify the calculation), and their numbers double every 20 years, in 200 years there will be 1 trillion non-whites. In 400 years, there will be 1 quadrillion non-whites.

b) If there are 1 million AIDS cases in the world, and the number doubles every 12 months, and every case takes an average of 5 years to die, there will be nobody left alive in the world by A.D. 2020.

It is obvious that these two extrapolations contradict each other, and that projection b) is just about the only possibility of forestalling projection a).

Regarding a), it has been calculated by computer that, at the present rate of increase, the total mass of non-white humanity will equal the mass of the earth by A.D. 3530, and will expand to fill the whole known universe (15 billion light years across) by A.D. 6826. According to the liberals and race-mixers, this universe of parasitic scum are all *"equal to us"*. They must all be provided with a modern standard of living at our expense, but they owe us nothing in return.

Regarding b), it is not exactly true that NO ONE would be left alive: AIDS is a communicable disease of the Negro race, the non-white races, the racially mixed, and all persons that mix with Negroes (Hispanics, Jews, race-mixers, drug addicts, homosexuals, etc).

Among whites, it is estimated that 5% of Italians and 14% of Swedes are in fact racially immune to AIDS. They are said to possess the G2-fast gene, exclusive to certain members of the White Race and providing full immunity if passed on by both parents.

Since AIDS is a disease of minority groups, the only concern of the liberals, predictably enough, is to protect their "civil rights". Carriers must therefore be exempt from all laws applying to the carriers of other diseases (such as syphilis or typhoid). Insurance companies must be prohibited from asking any questions designed to determine whether or not an individual may or may not be a carrier. All laws against homosexual activity, no matter how lenient, must be abolished. Negroes must be encouraged to screw white girls at all costs. *No problem!*

Liberalism is a form of progressive mental illness which may be defined as a form of moral coprophilia. The liberals will do anything – ANYTHING – even die horribly – rather than abandon the philosophy of human equality. AIDS carriers must be protected from discrimination; they must be included; they must be integrated; we must overcome our reaction of fear and rejection. *No problem!*

In 1991, in the university city of Coimbra, Portugal, the editor of a student newspaper wrote an article in which he asserted that 5% of all African students had tested positive for AIDS (correct percentage of African carriers: probably 20-30 %). The result was a panic in which Africans were kicked out of their lodgings and refused service in cafes. Eating utensils used by Africans were smashed.

The response of the liberals was typical: the student editor was expelled from school, and the problem was declared solved. *No problem!*

The only problem, say the liberals, is persuading people to use condoms (a device believed, in normal use, to be only 70-90% in preventing pregnancy, and which certainly cannot prevent the passing of a much smaller virus). *No problem!*

In Germany and Luxembourg, kindergartners were compelled to colour posters *saying "Liebe geht durch die Gummi, AIDS nicht"* ("Love goes through the rubber, AIDS doesn't"), an injunction which will presumably be kept in mind by the millions of public-spirited Turkish and Congolese pimps, drug pushers, and rapists. *No problem!*

Freud believed that there was a connection between repression and neurosis. Perhaps this is why our Western *"democracies"* are the most neurotic societies in the history of the world, characterized by an all-pervading atmosphere of nameless fear. The possession of heroin was legalized in Holland and Spain, while the sale of chewing tobacco and snuff became a crime in Belgium, Britain, and Ireland. *Tobacco products cause cancer, a disease which isn't even catching. That's terrible!*

The worship of homosexuals was made a *de facto* state religion despite their known role as major vectors of numerous diseases, including an incurable, fatal, symptomless illness, while hysterical demands were being made that *"genetically engineered foods"* be specifically labelled or even prohibited. The importation of such foods was actually prohibited in Luxembourg and Austria, in an atmosphere of media panic and emergency legislation. *You might eat something with genetically engineered soybeans in it! That's terrible!*

[Note: Actually, the anti-genetic-engineering people were quite right, but note that we are only allowed to worry about things as long as they are purely theoretical. When they materialize, they are ignored and something else is invented. A panic a day keeps the half-wits at bay.]

Liberalism and AIDS are the collision between an immovable object and an irresistible force. In attempting to contain the explosion, the liberals are only increasing its violence. The Revolution is coming. You can join us, and set up an authoritarian system of "Applied Racial Science", which means National Socialism, or you can die.

Since AIDS promises to wipe out the race-mixers, it follows that AIDS is the white man's best friend. The way things are going, we might end up alone on the planet – reduced in numbers, perhaps, but of distinctly higher quality, having learned a lesson or two.

It therefore follows that scientists and researchers working on a cure for AIDS are the world's worst threat to White Race survival, and should be dealt with as race traitors.

Liberals have never hesitated to take their principles to any extreme, no matter how irrational and insane. They instinctively fear that the inapplicability of the equality principle to any group of people threatens the principle itself, so it must be infinitely extended.

In the 1940s, the liberals told us there was *"No Difference"* between Jews and non-Jews. It became a crime to say that Jews hijacked the country and caused the war. It became "Nazi propaganda" to say that the gas chambers were an invention of Allied propaganda.

In the 1950s and 60s, the liberals told us there was *"No Difference"* between the races. It became a crime to *"discriminate"*, even when the Negro *"Master Race"* robbed, raped, and beat up our friends and relatives and wrecked our schools and neighbourhoods.

Since sexual differences are a reminder of racial differences, the liberals told us there was *"No Difference"* between men and women. It became a crime in France to advertise for "air hostesses".

Since national differences are a reminder of racial differences, the liberals told us there was *"No Difference"* between nationalities. It became a crime in Holland to advertise for job applicants who could speak Dutch.

Since the differences between homo and heterosexuals are a reminder of the differences between men and women, which in turn are a reminder of racial and national differences, the liberals told us there was *"No Difference"* between homo and heterosexuals. It became a crime to discriminate against homosexuals.

It then transpired that 50% of the homosexuals in San Francisco (to cite only one example) were already infected. The liberals were undaunted. They took their principle one step further. They told us there was *"No Difference"* between AIDS carriers and non-carriers, because only 10% of all carriers were developing the disease. *No problem!* It became a crime to discriminate against AIDS carriers. *"Closing Your Doors"* to the carriers of a fatal, incurable, and contagious illness! *How pitiless! How cruel!*

It then transpired that nearly 100% of AIDS carriers were developing the disease, sooner or later (regardless of all the "Living With AIDS" propaganda, etc.).

The liberals were undaunted. As always, they took their principle one step further. They told us there was *"No Difference"* between homosexuals who had already developed the disease, and others who hadn't (so far). It became a crime in Great Britain and elsewhere to fire terminally ill AIDS cases from their jobs.

It is now known that carriers are developing the disease at a rate of 100%, and dying at a rate of 100% (unless something else kills them first; usually the cause of death is falsified by attributing it to pneumonia or TB; the bright side is that the longer they live, the more people they infect).

This puts the liberals in a quandary. To be logically consistent, they must now argue that there is *"No Difference"* between homosexuals who are still alive, and others who have already died of the disease; that there is *"No Difference"* between the living and the dead.

This suggests the possibility of "Integration" with dead people.

Integration may take place in two directions: the liberals can dig up their dead friends and "integrate" with them (in the privacy of their own homes) – which is impossible since AIDS victims are always cremated – or the liberals can be "bussed" to the cemeteries and "integrated" with their dead friends there. We prefer the latter option.

This "solves" the problem. Since integration is a civil matter, the safeguards of criminal law do not apply. Integration may be "Hazardous to Your Health", but it is not a matter of criminal law.

Thus, all we need do, when the Revolution comes, is issue an "Integration Order", followed, upon failure to comply, by an "Implementation Order", to be carried out within 24 hours (plus costs).

A disclaimer: I am not saying that scientists working for an AIDS cure should be hunted down and killed, like abortionists – that would be murder. Murder is against the law. That is out of the question. But they can be... *"implemented"*.

After all, the liberals themselves have taught us that when we take something and give it a different name, it becomes something different, for example, that "Affirmative Action" is not discrimination, or that a foetus is not a "human being".

* * *

Thus far it would appear that AIDS is failing to live up to its promises, so brightly announced 15 or even 20 years ago; but it works in a mysterious way its wonders to perform. 15 years ago, it was calculated in the United States and Germany that 0.5% of all potential Army recruits were already infected; worldwide, that would be 30 million people. It was then discovered in anonymous public hospital emergency room testing that probably 25% of all male Negroes in New York City aged 20-35 were already infected. American Negroes are believed to be acquiring new cases at 14 times the rate of whites, and to be 5 times as infectious. Between 8 and 10 years ago, the AIDS infection rate in Central Africa (Rwanda-Burundi, etc.) was estimated at 50%, while in Southern Africa (Rhodesia, Malawi, Zambia, etc.) it was estimated at 20-25%. It is believed to be 13% in South Africa right now. The infection rate in the Congo is now believed to have approached 100% (!!!). This is not so unlikely as it may appear; the rate of infection among *voluntarily tested* members of the South African Defence Forces about 5 years ago was reliably stated to have been 89%. Similar statistics are available for Zambia and Rhodesia [a.k.a. Zimbabwe]. In the United States, 52% cases of all new cases are believed to involve non-whites; over 80% of all cases are now believed to involve blacks, Hispanics, drug addicts, race mixers, faggots, etc.

In 2001, the prestigious Robert Koch Institute in Germany estimated that "up to" 40% of *all Africans* were infected, but that the infection rate among homosexuals in Germany was far higher.

Let us assume that there are only 25 million carriers in the world (an estimate which must be viewed as absurdly conservative, since it is officially admitted that 13 million Africans have already died, an estimate which must, again, be viewed as absurdly conservative in view of the deliberate official policy of distortion of all information relating to the topic, and since it is simultaneously claimed that entire African villages have lost all their adults, that all the surviving children in those villages are AIDS orphans, that entire rural districts have become depopulated, etc. etc.).

Let us further assume that every AIDS carrier infects only ONE other person over a period of 2 years, and never anyone else – an another absurdly conservative assumption (Rock Hudson, for example, is believed to have infected hundreds of people although he knew he was dying of the disease) – the total number of infected persons will reach 6.4 BILLION PEOPLE in only 16 years, if not much sooner. That is the mathematical result of doubling the number 25 million 8 times over.

Assuming that there are 100 million carriers, which is probably far more realistic, the figure of 6.4 billion AIDS carriers will be reached in only 6 doublings. The question now arises: Can the AIDS infection rate double 8, or even 6, times in 16 years? The answer is that it appears to have done so in many areas already. In Massachusetts, in 1982, there were only 45 AIDS cases in the entire state. 12 years later, there were 10,000 AIDS cases, i.e., the number 45 doubled 8 times = 90, 180, 360, 720, 1440, 2880, 5760, 11,520 cases. 10,000 AIDS cases in Massachusetts doubled ANOTHER 8 times (i.e., in 12 MORE years) would be 12.8 million AIDS cases in the Commonwealth of Massachusetts alone. That is the effect of exponential doubling.

It should be borne in mind that any self-respecting crack addict or homosexual should be able to infect as least one or two people every other drunken weekend, while it takes a good 13 years for even the most sexually active Negro to reproduce and breed another Negro to reproduction/rapist age (i.e., two generations in 26 years).

It may be objected that the population of the world may well double while the AIDS carriers in question (i.e., the Congolese aforesaid, whether resident in the Congo or the idiot Kingdom of Belgium) are still alive, but many of these children will undoubtedly be carriers; even in this case, one more doubling, and the total number of infected persons will reach 12.8 billion.

How long does it take to infect one person with AIDS? That's how fast the total number can double in theory.

In *The War of the Worlds* by H.G. Wells, Martian invaders conquer the earth with death rays and poison gas, only to be destroyed by the earth's bacteria. The AIDS infection rate will undoubtedly explode as it becomes increasingly difficult to avoid infected persons (as with leprosy or TB). When one considers that AIDS-Related Complex is not even counted as AIDS, although it is caused by the same virus; that we are concerned only with carriers, and not fully developed cases, since the carriers will inevitably die unless something else kills them first; and that the longer they live, the more people they will can infect, the picture becomes almost optimistic. The idiocy of the liberals is playing into our hands in this way, if no other. Last but not least, many other "new, improved" diseases, such as West Nile Virus, Ebola Virus, galloping gangrene, Legionnaire's Disease, Marburg virus, etc. are also said to be appearing at the rate of 1 per year. Who says there's no order in the universe? That these new viruses appear to have killed very few people so far should not cause us to despair. To this must be added the scenario of trillions of dollars of bad debt in the world, i.e., there will not be the money to keep AIDS carriers alive artificially, or to treat all their other diseases. The AIDS virus is continually mutating, and appears quite likely to become increasingly resistant to drugs. (What we really need is for it to become more contagious, but that is possible as well.)

The phenomenon of exponential doubling is also the basis for many gambling schemes, the most successful of which is probably the one dignified with the name, in gambling parlance, of the *"paroli mise en arrière"*, i.e., doubling your bet when you are winning, then withdrawing part of the bet. For example, you are betting on black in roulette. You try to win three bets in a row, leaving the bet on the table, then withdraw the bet if you win, and go back to betting the minimum. For example, if you bet one dollar 3 times in a row, and lose, you have lost 3 dollars. If you WIN three times in a row, you have won 7 dollars (i.e., there are now 8 dollars on the table in front of you, but one of the them was already yours). If you *lose* 4 bets in a row, you have lost 4 dollars, but if you WIN 4 bets in a row, you have won 15 dollars (i.e., there are now 16 dollars on the table in front of you, but one of them was already yours). This can be quite spectacular in the short term. In the long run, of course, you will do no better than the law of averages, minus the house percentage, i.e., you will lose. Keep in mind that the table limit will probably be 25 times the minimum bet, 25 dollars if you are betting one dollar.

Albert Einstein advocated doubling your bet when you are losing, i.e., after 6 bets of one dollar, you will be betting 32 dollars to win 1 dollar (!!!), which will not work anyway, because of the table limit of 25 times the minimum bet, i.e., 25 dollars. This means that if you lose 5 bets in a row, you're finished. This technique is called the *"paroli mise en avant",* and the casinos love it. That is one reason why I do not believe in the Theory of Relativity: I have no confidence in its author as a gambler.

[Note: Einstein is known to have been a genius who had no real common sense, and the above is only one example. Mathematicians say that there are *no* mathematical errors in the Theory of Relativity, and that it is a waste of time trying to find any. The fallacy lies in assuming that if something is true mathematically, it is also true in reality. For example, Einstein claims that if a spaceship travels for 1 million years to a distant planet and back, on the planet Earth, one million years will have passed; but the travellers on the spaceship will only be one day older! This is like saying that if Los Angeles and New York are 2000 miles apart, and my car can go 100 miles an hour, then I can drive cross-country and back in only 40 hours! Obviously, the Theory must contain some truth, or it wouldn't be possible to blow up the world with all the bombs invented by Jews for the express purpose of exterminating the Germans, then smuggled by Jews to the Communists for 55 years. I have no quarrel with any other aspect of the Theory.]

White refugees from South Africa tell me that AIDS is having no impact, because the blacks breed faster than the disease can kill them off, but in view of the above, that seems a very short-term view. Of course, if the white South Africans had had a little bit more courage, intelligence, and determination in the first place, they would not be refugees now – begging charity from the same countries that hate them and that destroyed South Africa. There is order in the universe. *"Those who do not wish to fight in this world of eternal struggle do not deserve to live."*

P.S. Q: *What's "gay" stand for?*
A: *"Got AIDS Yet?"*

* * *

It is now officially admitted that, in the past 20 years, 750,000 Americans have contracted AIDS, and that 450,000 of them have died, most of them presumably black or (that Holy of Holies) homosexual. This is 10 times the number of whites murdered by blacks since the "Civil Rights" movement began, but only 1% of the number of white children murdered by Jewish, lesbian, or homosexual abortionists since 1973. Fortunately, Jews have very high abortion rates, and relatively high AIDS rates. In the "white Caribbean", AIDS is now the No. 1 cause of death among all persons aged 15 to 55. Similar statistics have been reported from certain American cities with regards to American blacks. Presumably the situation in places like Haiti or Darkest Africa is far worse. It is now admitted that *25 million* Africans have died, as against the mere 13 million claimed just a few months ago. Of course, the concern of the liberals, as always, is directed exclusively towards homosexuals, blacks, and Africans.

Although all these figures are probably so unreliable as to be almost worthless, the figure of 100 million carriers in the world, mentioned above, must be assumed to be realistic. What is more, if we assume 20 healthy carriers for every person who has already died – an extremely conservative assumption – there must be *at least* 500 million carriers in the world. At this rate, the end is already in sight. There is order in the universe.

It should be noted that if every AIDS carrier infected *one* other person every *week* (which is quite possible, since carriers are highly infectious immediately after infection, before the appearance of the antibodies), the world would be wiped out in only 9 *months* (plus the time required for all the carriers to die).

That this is far from being the case, proves that even the most conservative of assumptions can still be devastating long term: the indications are that each carrier, on average, infects ONE person only once every two YEARS – a snail's pace in view of the mobility and promiscuity of some of the target populations involved. Yet even this is evidently sufficient (see above).

10 years ago, it was claimed that 1 million cases of AIDS-Related Complex in the United States did not constitute "AIDS", and were not included in the statistics, yet ARC is caused by the AIDS virus. New infection rates among white homosexuals were recently estimated at approximately 4% per year; among black homo- and bisexuals, 14.7%! (Prison inmates claim that *all* blacks are bisexual,

although precisely what this means when blacks are not in prison is far from clear; probably 25% of all young black males are in prison at any given time. In South Africa, 85% of all prison inmates are believed to have been sodomized within 48 hours of arrival.) Life expectancy among (non-incarcerated) lesbians in the United States is now estimated at only 45 years; *only 2% of American male homosexuals even reach the age of 65, with murder rates 125 times higher than the general population!* Maybe they know something the liberals don't know.

Furthermore, the admitted figure of 450,000 deaths from AIDS in the United States in 20 years is almost certainly too low, and should probably be doubled. This means that the number of AIDS deaths – *not just carriers or cases, but actual deaths* – has doubled 9, and almost certainly 10, times in 20 years. Another 8 doublings will wipe out the United States. This means that the political systems under which we live will be destroyed within 16 to 20 years at most, and the enemies of revisionism and the White Race will die horribly. The wages of sin are death, now as never before. Nature is Nazi.

"And Joshua said unto them, Fear not, nor be dismayed, be strong and of good courage: for thus shall the LORD do to all your enemies against whom ye fight."

– Josh: 10:25

* * *

According to the Center for Contagious Disease Control in Atlanta about two years ago, 749,041 Americans had already died of AIDS (a figure which is undoubtedly far too low, since most deaths from AIDS are attributed to pneumonia, with 18,000 *official* AIDS deaths per year) – while 65 MILLION Americans (a quarter of the population) suffer from *incurable* S.T.D.s – mostly genital herpes, which is extremely contagious. (This disease alone infects an estimated 50% of all black women in America.)

Since persons with S.T.D.s are far more susceptible to AIDS, the explosion point is a question of time. Added to the 50 million deaths from abortion since 1973, this means that *the "sexual revolution" is one of the greatest catastrophes in human history, comparable to Communism or the Second World War.*

Woe to thee Babylon, that art to be destroyed.

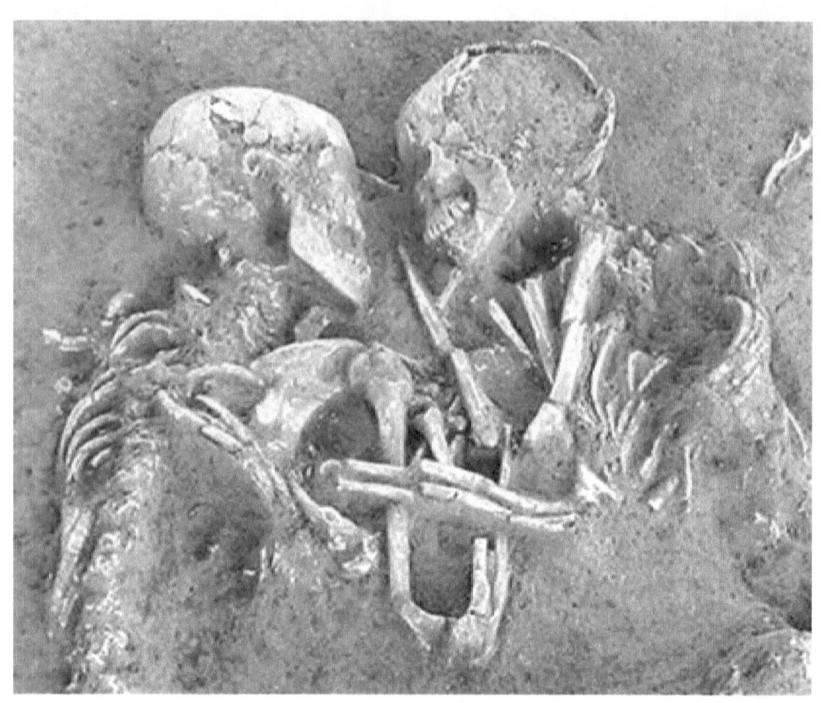

* * *

African Children Orphaned by AIDS

The Associated Press – July 3, 1999
Deborah Hastings, Associated Press Writer

LUSAKA, Zambia (AP) – The younger ones sit cross-legged, quietly waiting, like schoolchildren expecting the story hour.

The teenagers, two feet away, are stone drunk from guzzling buckets of 100-proof, homemade beer called kachasu, and *sniffing jekem – fermented human feces scraped from sewer pipes. They stab at each other with screwdrivers and swing lengths of metal pipe.*

It is dark and cold and about 40 filthy, barefoot street children gather on the dirt and concrete strip that divides this capital's main thoroughfare, waiting for Rodgers Mwewa and his promise of food. The wait is long and a melee has erupted over a stolen pair of shoes.

Into the middle of this mess wades Mwewa, a 28-year-old Zambian relief worker with more heart than common sense. Heedless of the danger, he has assembled these children in the wide center of two-lane Cairo Road, which teems with speeding minibuses. The sidewalks are worked by pickpockets, some the very ones Mwewa has come to feed.

Some 90,000 children live on the streets of Zambia. Many are the sole survivors of families destroyed by HIV. This Southern African country of 9.5 million is home to the world's highest concentration of AIDS orphans, according to the United Nations. More than half of all Zambian children – an estimated 600,000 – have lost at least one parent, most to the epidemic.

The country's future is an abandoned, lost generation.

On this recent night, they fight each other for Mwewa's pots of stewed meat and nsima, a bread-like staple made from cornmeal that has the consistency of wallpaper paste. It fills hungry stomachs but provides little nutrition.

Zambia, a British colony until 1964, is one of the world's poorest countries and one of the hardest hit by AIDS. Death is so common, coffins are sold out of brightly colored vans parked on roadsides.

Downtown Lusaka is a ragtag collection of plywood market stalls selling everything from bananas to hand-woven cloth. Its main drag is punctuated by an occasional high-rise, meagerly stocked department stores and a string of pizza and chicken joints. Their greasy fumes mix with the smells of diesel and dirt.

Foreigners are a rarity on Lusaka streets and are viewed by these desperate children as walking bags of cash. The presence of a foreign reporter and a woman from the Dutch embassy escalates the nighttime frenzy on Cairo Road.

"Please madame, please madame, give me money," they cry, with imploring looks that are sometimes practiced, sometimes predatory, but always pitiable.

The teen-agers sniff petrol, aerosol cans, anything to remain numb. Their feet are calloused to rawhide. Their clothes hang from bodies stunted by malnutrition.

Steven Chipili is 13 but looks 8. He is scooping meat and nsima with his fingers. He wears only a dirt-encrusted sweater stretching to his knees.

Something is definitely wrong with him.

He wallows on the median strip, laughing demonically, as if possessed, at images only he sees. According to Mwewa, Steven was perfectly normal before he ran from police who tried to shake him down for a pocketful of panhandled money.

He was beaten, kicked and left in the street. Mwewa found him the next day and took him to the hospital. That was a few months ago.

"The boy has not been right since," Mwewa says.

Last year, in the northern Copperbelt, where the mines are giving out and thousands are jobless, Steven's parents died of AIDS within four months of each other. He had no one else. So he hopped a freight train to Lusaka. More children arrive each day and quickly learn to survive on charity, thievery and prostitution. Girls and boys who should be in grade school sell their small bodies in order to eat.

Winter is approaching in the Southern Hemisphere, and on Cairo Road, the night gets later and chillier. The teen-agers and the younger ones are now a swarming mob. They dart in and out of traffic, then grab Mwewa and surround the embassy worker's car.

"Just go!" screams one of Mwewa's volunteers. Mwewa is stubborn and stays. He fruitlessly tries to calm children who are screaming and tugging at the car doors.

Tyson, a 16-year-old boy nicknamed for the power of his punch, flails and cries in pain. His jaw is swollen to the size of a lemon and he wants a dentist. Now.

"Tomorrow," Mwewa says, trying to reason with a violent drunk.

"Tomorrow I will take you to the dentist."

Days later, Tyson is dead. The TV news reports that a security guard unleashed his dog on the boy while he was begging in front of a chicken restaurant. Tyson ran onto Cairo Road and into the path of a minibus. Mwewa spends 1.4 million kwacha on the funeral, about $600. Most of it comes from a Canadian relief organization donation.

Wouldn't that money better serve the living?

"What am I supposed to do?" he says. "It is our culture to give a good funeral."

Mwewa directs Fountain of Hope, a grassroots relief agency that barely lives up to its name. If current infection rates continue, the numbers of dead mothers and fathers will increase for at least 20 years, say international aid groups.

Average life expectancy here has plummeted from 56 to 37 years, according to the U.S. Census Bureau. About 20 percent of the population – an estimated one in five adults – is infected. The American rate is 0.57 percent.

Mwewa has a geology degree and used to work in the copper mines, once the backbone of the economy. "The chemicals were making me sick," he says, and so he quit. He turned to this work, compelled by what he saw on the streets.

The impoverished government can spend next to nothing on AIDS or its orphans.

It counts on foreign relief agencies to carry an impossible load. Fountain of Hope exists on piecemeal funding from such groups.

It is similar in neighboring Botswana, Namibia and Zimbabwe. Their struggling governments can't cope with the epidemic's merciless march across southern Africa, where the number of victims is highest.

There are exceptions. In Uganda, a government-funded education program is credited with decreasing infection rates.

Twelve years ago, Zambia's then-president, Kenneth Kaunda, tried to inspire a national campaign against AIDS by disclosing that his own 30-year-old son had died from the disease.

It had little effect. The disease is predominantly spread by heterosexuals and birth control is not embraced here. A family's social standing increases with the number of its children.

Zambia is steeped in tribal taboos and born-again Christianity. Few speak openly of sex or say the virus' name.

In the shantytowns, it is called "the slimming disease." In the villages, it is "this thing that has come."

No one knows how many orphans carry the virus. No one tests them because it would do no good. There is no treatment here. Even AZT, the most basic of AIDS drugs, is unaffordable in a country where $50 a month is considered good pay.

Zambia's few orphanages are full. In the villages, children who have lost their parents and most other relatives are bundled aboard buses to Lusaka. Effectively disowned, they are told to find help in the big city.

"I put this kid on the bus and I say 'Go find your uncle.' But where are they going to find this uncle? They don't. He doesn't exist," says Louis Mwewa.

Louis Mwewa, no relation to Rodgers, heads Children in Need, an umbrella network representing the few orphan groups such as Fountain of Hope.

"We have to do something. But even the few of us who do something, we are reduced to beggars. I have to run up and down to get money, and all of us, we're going to the same places," he said.

The government closed Fountain of Hope's drop-in center because of a cholera outbreak. So the group moved into the Kamwala shantytown, where a new school is being built. Rodgers Mwewa needs about $25,000 to finish the building and doesn't have it.

So far, only the foundation has been poured. Classes are held outdoors, on wobbling benches that tip every five minutes, dumping their occupants into giggling heaps. Orphans are taught English and rudimentary math on blackboards propped against jacaranda trees. One day, it is hoped, these children will pass the entrance exam for Lusaka schools.

But it will take them years, and Zambian schools are not free. Costs range from $10 a year for the younger ones to about $30 for the oldest. Fountain of Hope also tries, diplomatically, to teach children about safe sex. Instructors use soda bottles to demonstrate how to use a condom. But, said teacher Brian Mulenga, the lectures don't go far with 8-year-old boy prostitutes.

"Why don't they make condoms for children?" the youngsters inquire.

"They are too big and they fall off." Mulenga laughs, then snaps into seriousness.

"They really asked this," he said.

Catherine Phiri, 8, has lost both parents to AIDS. She lives in Kamwala with a charity woman who takes in orphans. She has no brothers or sisters. She doesn't even remember how she got here.

For days, she wears the same filthy blue sweater. She trudges to school on a dirt path, her bare feet sending up small clouds of dust. Always, she must pass the whitewashed concrete hut where a radio blasts South African music and leering men without jobs drink the day away.

At the school grounds, Rodgers Mwewa translates Catherine's mumbled answers in Nyanga, one of Zambia's prevailing tribal tongues. It is difficult to pull an answer or a smile from this girl. Her tiny face is hard as flint.

What does she want to be when she grows up?

She hangs her head and plucks weeds from the ground. Mwewa asks again. Finally, in a voice barely audible, she answers.

Mwewa's face is clouded by defeat.

"She wants to be a cleaning woman," he says.

Just outside Lusaka, in the slums of Matero, local women banded together in 1991 to help an ever-increasing number of orphans. They named themselves Kwasha Mukwenu, which means "help your friend." They have registered more than 2,000 orphans, but can only feed about 100 a day. The women also clothe and send some of these children to school with money badgered from relief agencies and raised by selling baked goods and batik cloth.

Under the leadership of Elizabeth Ngoma, a large woman with an infectious laugh, Kwasha Mukwenu tries to find homes for the orphans, either with distant relatives or families willing to take in strays. In some houses, grandmothers care for as many as 17 children.

For most of these children, the meal eaten here is their only one of the day.

As in every shantytown, the people of Matero walk. Cars are unaffordable. So the arrival of a truck draws a crowd.

Inside the Catholic church, some 60 children sit quietly on straw mats, balancing green plastic plates laden with nsima by the women of Kwasha Mukwenu. The youngsters smile and shyly wave, but never stop chewing.

Emanuel Daka, 14, lives in a nearby house with his mother, brother and sister. His father is dead of AIDS. His mother is dying of tuberculosis, one of Africa's most common opportunistic infections from HIV.

He is in sixth grade. English is his favorite subject, though he cannot speak it yet. He dreams of being a priest.

"I want to preach and tell the people the truth about these people who are dying of AIDS," he says through an interpreter.

He is asked how he lives with the knowledge that his mother will soon die. He stares at the floor. Minutes pass. "I feel very bad," he answers flatly. "I am going to be left alone."

He is surrounded by the Kwasha Mukwenu women, who nod and continue talking and laughing. Death is nothing new. The women produce receipts for medicine to document their work. They need more money, they say. They cannot help every child.

Suddenly, one of them gasps. "Oh," she cries. "Look at him."

Tears are streaming down Emanuel's face. The thought of his mother's death has overwhelmed him.

Mulenga Kapwebwe sees children like Emanuel every day. She is the daughter of Zambia's first vice president and a worker with California-based Project Concern International. It teaches Fountain of Hope the Byzantine skills of writing grant applications and soliciting donors.

In her world, 5-year-olds have sexually transmitted diseases. If a man will pay more for sex without a condom, so be it. The child must eat today. Tomorrow has not arrived.

"There is no age of innocence anymore," she says. "You have to get used to certain things."

Three days later, on a beautiful evening just before sunset, Rodgers Mwewa walks into a backyard party attended by international relief workers. There is a buffet, an open bar, soft music and polite conversation. Mwewa has come straight from Fountain of Hope, where his long, depressing day ended with the arrival of a raped little girl.

Falling apart over each injustice does no good. Mwewa can do nothing more for the girl until tomorrow. To do this work requires not only compassion, but also the ability to turn it off.

He looks toward the bar and covets the numbing effect of a stiff drink. The 8-year-old orphan stumbled into Fountain of Hope as he was leaving. She was attacked in daylight while walking alone in Kamwala. Mwewa and his volunteers cleaned her up. She was taken to the hospital.

Now he struggles to shake her image. One detail refuses to budge.

"She had blood running down her leg," he says in a soft voice that is swallowed up by party chatter.

"Every day I praise God for AIDS... the White Race will come back, stronger than ever... you're not supposed to apologize for being right."
— J.B. Stoner

"¡Viva la muerte!"

— José Millán Astray

1995–2003

ON THE BANKING SYSTEM

Revolution Without Guns

I will now discuss the question: "Why go to prison for robbing armoured cars to finance the Revolution, when there are legal ways of stealing much more money?"

We sometimes forget that stealing is legal. Of course, it is called unpleasant names, such as: breach of contract, gross negligence, wilful negligence, insolvency, and debt. But it is legal.

There is no imprisonment for debt. I know people who have stolen millions of dollars and who will never spend a day in court, except for preliminary hearings, etc. Of course, they have all kinds of lawsuits against them, but that doesn't matter. They stole legally.

Legal stealing falls into three categories:
a) the nigger method
b) the white man method
c) the Jew method, the latter being the ultimate in perfection.

Method a) consists of saying "Gimme fi' dollahs til payday", and then saying, "Cain't whup me, doan' git it". That is crude, but legal.

Method b) consists of forming a corporation (which need only exist on paper), paying your initial invoices very quickly, establishing a line of credit with a variety of suppliers (payment within 60 days of invoice, etc. etc.), taking large orders, selling off the goods, declaring insolvency, and forming another corporation. That is legal (if you've got a smart lawyer it's legal).

Method c) consists of becoming a banker.

A banker is essentially an agent who borrows at one rate of interest and lends at another, the difference between the two interest rates constituting his profit.

If I borrow one billion dollars at 6 ¾ % interest and re-lend it at 7%, the difference between the two interest rates is 2.5 million dollars a year. The ¼% represents a slight increase in risk only. If I assume a much larger risk (for example, a much longer term loan or a shady borrower), I can mark it up 2 or 3%, which means 20-30 million dollars a year, ten times as much. In some countries, you can open a "bank" with as little as $1,000,000 in cash (called "Paid-In Capital"), maybe even $100,000. If I collect the interest for one year, I am set up for life.

And if you default, the bank is a corporation. I have no personal liability. I will declare bankruptcy. They can't take my house or my car, let them take the computers and the office furniture.

I don't even care whether you can ever repay, because it's not my money, I borrowed it. All I want is the interest. The loan contract says you've got to repay, but that's okay, I'll loan you the money to repay it with. I'll even loan you the money to pay the interest (that is called "Extending New Credits").

It is important to understand this mentality, because without it, every government and supra-governmental institution in the world would collapse in a second.

Any self-respecting tax haven (and to a lesser extent, any financial district anywhere) has dozens of banks employing perhaps half a dozen people each, in just 2 or 3 rooms in an ordinary apartment house. These "banks" have no cash. If you went in with a machine gun to rob the joint you'd get about fifteen dollars. They have no depositors. They do all their business by wire.

Now, before I collapse, of course, all these worthless loans I have extended will be entered on my books as assets, and will be used as collateral for further loans to me.

Pay careful attention now. If interest rates are at 7%, a 20-year loan (for example, a government bond) will be worth nearly face value as collateral. If interest rates rise to 8%, the face value of that same bond will fall by roughly 1/7th, because the same amount of money can now buy a bond yielding 8% (one seventh more).

If interest rates then fall ¼%, the face value of that same bond will rise by ¼ of 1/7th, or 2.8 % (in practice, much less, because of commissions, expenses, taxes, etc.).

Since this is a large price movement in long-term bonds, such bonds can be bought on credit for about 1% deposit (called "Margin").

When I get into a jam (called a "Liquidity Crisis") because of all these worthless loans I have extended, threatening a depression, in comes the argument for central banking. The central bank will act as the "Lender of Last Resort"; it will "Inject Liquidity into the Banking System".

By some curious coincidence, the central bankers, who will happen to be friends of mine, will also have centralized control over interest rates.

This means that the market value of trillions of dollars of securities will rise and fall by an exact mathematical formula according to a decision taken in utter secrecy by a very small number of people, who are my personal friends.

If you knew for a fact that the Prime Rate would be lowered by ¼ of a point next Tuesday, you could probably double your money in 2 days speculating in long-term Treasury Bonds. We hear a great deal about inside dealing in the stock market, but nothing about inside trading on the bond markets. (Related stocks and commodities, such as land, agricultural products, etc. will also rise and fall at the same time, but in a manner much more difficult to quantify and/or predict.)

In addition, central control of interest rates offers all kinds of advantages, for example, the opportunity to cause depressions.

Depressions are often considered a failure of the financial system, but that is not so. Depressions represent the success of the system. They are a requirement of the system. They make the system successful. They create a buying opportunity for speculators and act to liquidate debt.

The only problem is that liquidating trillions of dollars worth of government debt means liquidating a currency and government. This is far more complex than simply liquidating a corporation. To do so successfully requires a revolution or the loss of a war, and preferably both. No revolutionary government will pay principal and interest on the debts of a system it has overthrown. But you need a new government and a new currency.

So, the situation is as follows. The bankers need a revolution to repudiate their debts, so they can start the borrowing merry-go-round again. We have a "Revolution For Sale". I propose a deal.

They "throw the fight", we take over the government, they repudiate all U.S. dollar debts, and begin re-borrowing, blaming us for the repudiation. They get a lucrative cut in the printing and credit expansion of our own new, equally worthless new currency (hereinafter referred to as the "Imitation Jewbucknik", or JIMBUCKNIK), in the trading of our own new, equally worthless government bonds (known as JIMBONDS), and centralized control of interest rates under our own new, Revolutionary Government.

They are happy, we are happy.

Then we break our word to them and shoot all the bankers.

1991–2007

Limericks on the Banking System

I went drinking with an Englishman who told me about a friend named Frank, made redundant by a bank. I said, "That sounds like a limerick". Two days later, I sent him the following:

(to be read with ultra-snooty British accent)
[trumpet fanfare]

A lowly accounts clerk named Frank
Was employed by a reputable Bank
When rendered redundant
By crises abundant
He stumbled and staggered and sank.

My God! said the downtrodden Frank
I've slaved 30 years for the Bank
This "crawft" I have "mawstawd"
So some scheming "bawstawd"
Can swindle me out of my rank.

By Jove! said the crafty young Frank
I'll wreak my revenge on the Bank
The entries I'll alt-awh
And fill up Gibralt-awh
And Caicos and Caiman and Manx.

The vengeful young villain named Frank
Embezzled so much that it stank
He fiddled the ledge-awhs
Of swapp-awhs and hedge-awhs
And wired the swag to his bank.

Hi-Ho! Said the thief as he drank
I've diddled and fiddled the Bank
In silken pi-jawhmas
I'll haunt the Ba-hawhmas
With a sporty young bird on my flank.

My God! said the head of the Bank
We've swindled the world, but not Frank
He who laughs lawh-stest
And swindles the fawh-stest
Can buy off the law and live swank.

2008

ON CHRISTIANITY

Forgiveness, Christian Style

I have decided to renounce National Socialism and become a Bible-believing Christian. The story of this extraordinary conversion is as follows.

War is a universal constant of human history. Since people fight even when there is no need to do so, and since races and nationalities are being mixed on an unprecedented scale, and since natural resources are running out, it follows that the 21st century will be an epoch of unprecedented racial and national conflict.

Thus, if we wish to survive, instead of allowing other people to kill us, we must be guided by a philosophy which makes a virtue of mass killing.

Now, if the revisionists are correct, and there is no doubt that they are, the National Socialists did not advocate or practice mass killing (except as reprisals in guerrilla warfare) and apparently have very little experience in the matter.

Further, it is obvious that National Socialism offers no justification for mass killing, but that Christianity does.

For instance:

– 3 Turks (the children of a convicted pimp and indicted drug pusher) burnt to death in a suburb of Lübeck, Germany, allegedly by Nazis.
RESULT: Indignation from Christians.

– 926 adult Germans and 28 children killed by foreigners the year before, including a family of five Germans killed by a Turk in another suburb of the same city that same year.
RESULT: No reaction from Christians.

– 300,000 white Christian children burnt to death at Dresden by white Christian bomber pilots on a Christian holiday – Shrove Tuesday – Ash Wednesday, 1945, when it was coldly calculated that the maximum number of children would be on the streets in their Carnival costumes trying to forget the war.
RESULT: No need to apologise. No need for the Queen of

England to lay a wreath, not even a single rose, on the monument: an inscription referring to the British role in this tragedy was chiselled away.

– 300,000 Iraqis burnt to death in a carnival of killing by white Christian bomber pilots.
RESULT: Overwhelming endorsement by Christian churches as a fulfilment of Biblical prophecy.

– 200,000 British soldiers cornered at Dunkirk and allowed to escape because Hitler was an admirer of the British.
RESULT: No appreciation from Christians.

Christian tourists visit cities they have destroyed, burning hundreds of thousands of civilians to death, in Germany, Japan, Europe, and feel no guilt. Germans feel guilty for things they never attempted, or even thought of. Germans are fools.

Since National Socialism offers no justification for mass killing, and since Christians have the best philosophy of mass killing, it is not surprising that Christians are the world's best mass murderers, rivalled only by Jewish Communists.

A principal reason for the failure of National Socialism to attract adherents is its lack of hypocrisy. National Socialists state openly that conflict is a law of nature, and adopt a sporting attitude: may the better man win, may the best country win, may the better race win. Christianity suffers from no such defect.

Hitler said "The prerequisite for successful action is the courage and the will to be truthful." Christians know that truth is of no importance: what counts is doing the will of God (as interpreted by Christians).

God walks with me and talks with me and tells me I am his own. I was talking to Him just yesterday (incidentally He gave me a very nice autographed picture of Himself which is visible to those with great faith; make sure your cheque is good) and He tells me I have come into a considerable parcel of highly desirable real estate: the world. We are having trouble getting a clear title; there are squatters on the property (everybody else in the world); proceedings have been protracted (3,000 years); but there can be no doubt that I will come into my inheritance any day now.

In the meantime of course, legal technicalities aside, it is clear that the squatters have no moral right to occupy my property.

In the 16th century Spanish Christians exterminated the native population of Haiti through slave labour, and then discovered a tribe on a nearby island whom Columbus described as "loving each other as themselves". A peculiarity of this tribe of ignorant savages was their extraordinary devotion to the memory of their departed kinsfolk. The Spanish embarked 40,000 of them on board ship promising to transport them to "heavenly shores" where they would be reunited with their departed friends and relatives, and then took them to Haiti and slaved them to death, as a result of which the entire tribe became extinct.

As a National Socialist, I would consider this an example of the manner in which the idiocy of religious belief is exploited by criminals for material gain. But as a Bible-believing Christian, I can raise no objection. For is it not written, "Whomsoever the Lord our God shall drive out from before us, them will we possess" (Judges 11:24)?

Why should anyone feel guilty about a successful crime? For is it not written, "Remember the Lord thy God; for it is he that giveth thee power to get wealth" (Deut. 8:18)?

Let Hitler capture his enemies and let them go because he admires them; Christians know that their enemies are to be destroyed. For is it not written, "Spare ye not her young men; destroy ye utterly all her host" (Jeremiah 51:3)?

Christianity is a religion of race suicide (the New Testament) grafted on to a religion of racial and religious mass murder (the Old Testament). In the past, I attacked this as immoral, and was rebuked by Christians on the grounds that God is the source of all morality, His actions cannot be immoral.

I now accept this as correct, or putting it another way, one can just as easily take the murder bits for oneself, and preach the suicide bits to others; that's the Christian way: why not?

Let's now take Christ's famous injunction to castrate ourselves for the "Kingdom of Heaven's sake" (Matthew 19:12). It is sometimes alleged that the passage is a deliberate mistranslation by Jews working on the king James Bible, but that is not true. No one needs a Jew to translate New Testament Greek. St Origen castrated himself on the basis of the Greek text, but also had a knowledge of Hebrew. The Russian Orthodox sect of Skoptsy castrated themselves on the basis of the Russian and Romanian texts. The Latin text, translated by St. Augustine, is even more explicit than the English: "Et sunt eunuchi qui se ipsos castraverunt propter regnum caelorum."

The Catholic Church has consistently condemned the practice of self-castration while engaging in the castration of choirboys for centuries to sing soprano in the Sistine Chapel. The *1911 Encyclopaedia Britannica* calls eunuchs "the artistic glory and moral shame of the Papal choir".

Since the Pope was declared infallible in 1870 and since the trade in castrated choirboys continued until 1878 [The practice was prohibited in the Papal States in 1870 and the castrati were eliminated from the Papal choir by Pope Leo XIII in 1878. The last actual castration was reportedly performed on Alessandro Moreschi in 1865.], we may assume that the practice was stopped, not on moral grounds, but as a financial measure: it was illegal in the rest of Italy, so there were hefty bribes to be paid to middlemen and poor parents; in addition to which many boys died after surgery, giving rise to an unacceptable percentage of spoilt goods.

Thus it is the opinion of the highest authorities in Christendom – indeed an infallible authority – that while we may not castrate ourselves "for the Kingdom of Heaven's sake" we may castrate OTHERS "for the Kingdom of Heaven's sake".

Blessed are the meek, for they shall be enslaved, castrated and burnt alive by Christians.

Now if the practice was abolished on financial grounds it may presumably be re-instated (financial resources permitting). Perhaps it could be applied, in a spirit of Christian love and forgiveness, to the abortionists, mostly Jewish, who have killed 50 million children, mostly white, since 1973; to the homosexual rapists (virtually 100% negro) who infest our integrated prison system; to the government officials who integrated our prison system; to the millions of child molesters who infest our cities; to the lawyers, psychiatrists and judges who release them again to prowl our streets; to the pimps and promoters who peddle freaks like Prince and Michael Jackson as role models for our children, and to all those who got us into two World Wars and advocated the sterilisation of the German people.

There is another reason for my decision to come to Jesus. My mother died nine years ago and left two trusts for "the Christian education and maintenance" of my four children, attending Catholic schools.

Since the will calls for "joyful Bible study" (something impossible to define in a court of law), and since the trustee is a Bible-believing Christian (which is to say, a thief and a liar) we have never gotten a penny from either trust in nine years. Nobody's Bible study is ever joyful enough! Lawyers are useless; maybe Jesus can get me a buck or two.

1994

ON DEBT

Give Me Liberty or Give Me Debt

Did you ever wonder why new supermarkets are built right next door to supermarkets that have gone bankrupt?

It's because the money is borrowed. If I borrow 90% of the money for a project and make 10% per year, I have doubled my money. If it's not profitable, I repudiate the loan.

This probably accounts for 90% of all economic activity, most of which serves no purpose other than to destroy the environment and provide short-term employment for non-whites (until they get on welfare, which takes them a while).

The wonderful thing about debt is, no matter how much you have, you can always acquire more. All you have to do is promise to pay more interest.

If a small town wants to put in a sewer system, do they pay for it out of taxes? Of course not. They hold a bond drive. If interest rates are 4%, they apply the tax revenues to the interest for 25 years, and borrow 25 times as much money. To pay off the principle would require tax increases of thousands of percent.

This system makes everybody happy. The taxpayers get a sewer system they don't have to pay for and the lenders get a return backed by the "Taxing Power of the State". The insolvency of the system doesn't bother them.

Now, studies have shown that, to the average white idiot, the characters in his favourite TV programmes are more real to him than his own family and friends. He cares more about TV than the future of his own children. When he loses his job because his company has moved to China, and he can't get another because he is not a homo or some other species of protected wildlife, he uses his unemployment money to pay the light bill and watches more TV than ever.

There was no TV in South Africa until 1975, because they couldn't decide what language it was supposed to be in (Afrikaans or English). 20 years of TV was all it took to make the toughest whites in the world, the Boers, efface themselves from history like beer spilt on a bar.

This will only stop when there is no more money to pay the light bill. When that happens, the influence of TV will vanish in a second. Viewers all over the world will awaken as from a hypnotic trance (literally). This can only happen in a financial depression.

Thus, it is the duty of every racially aware person to bring about a depression as quickly as possible. That means we must all borrow as much money as possible.

Of course, it would be defeating the purpose of such an exercise to pay back the principal; that won't cause the debt bubble to burst. And it would be stealing to use the money for our own selfish pleasures (besides, anything we buy with our ill-gotten gains will be seized by bailiffs).

So, the trick is: We borrow the money from Jewish-owned finance companies promising to pay high rates of interest, divert the money to the racial struggle in cash contributions, then default on the loans.

If 1,000 racists borrow $1,000 each, that's one million dollars. Of course, that's not enough, because they can take us to small claims court. So we borrow $10,000. For $10,000 they have to hire a lawyer. That's 10 million Jew buckniks for the cause.

If it was logical for Pretty Boy Floyd to rob banks because the banks were going broke and the depositors were losing their dough, it is even more logical for white racists to rob finance companies, because they have no depositors. They borrow their money from your pension fund, sometimes even overnight. This is money you'll never see, because your company will declare insolvency and start a subsidiary in the "Pacific Rim countries" or Central America with the same name. The money is yours already. Why not take it?

Look in the paper. "$1,000 Over the Telephone", "$10,000 in 24 Hours", etc. *The system is begging to be ripped off.* All industry is being moved to China, and will eventually be nationalized. The financial advisers know this, but only care about short-term profit. To them, six months is a very long time. If the investment produces a total loss in 2 years or 5 years, they don't care, because they'll have sold their stock by then. When the Chinese get ready to blow up the world with technology we sold them, to be paid for using money we lent them (your money), the investment managers will re-invest in American armaments industries and manage their funds from a bomb shelter. Wars are Jews' harvests.

Just as whites can play jazz, but lack natural rhythm, we can also lie, cheat, and steal, even though we lack the innate cunning of the Jew. If anything, we lie better than the Jews, because our lies lack the mentally ill exaggerations which typify Jew lying. Look at the Gettysburg Address. Every sentence contains at least one lie, sometimes 2 or 3, but it has dignity. No Jew could lie like Lincoln.

One of the best con-men I ever knew was the son of the National Socialist consul in Barcelona. His technique was to take out large numbers of unsecured loans for small sums which were never repaid. He would agree to anything and sign anything. Proof that Aryans can compete with Jews in any field.

Now, the trick to robbing your creditors is, always owe at least 5 times your assets, and make sure your assets never exceed whatever it costs to sue you.

I know someone whose liabilities were absolutely phenomenal. He had assets of $50,000. He made an offer in compromise of $25,000 which was accepted. Why? Because it would have cost $50,000 to sue him, he would have spent the $50,000 defending himself, and there would have been nothing left to collect.

I know an accountant who stole 2 million dollars (this was in England, but the accounts were in dollars). There was a perfectly clear case against him. There were 60 witnesses, including myself; there were thousands of false accounting documents bearing his personal signature; there was an oral confession before 3 auditors; the man who helped him steal the money and divert it to other purposes (the man with the $50,000 in assets described above), turned Queen's evidence in return for civil immunity. The police recommended prosecution. The prosecutors delayed for 3 years because they couldn't be bothered with "such small cases", then dropped it because of the "age of the offence". The accountant's professional liability insurance wouldn't pay because "it didn't cover fraud", yet the opinion of the liability insurer that the accountant's actions constituted "fraud" was considered merely an "unproven allegation", so the same person is still practising as a Fellow of the Institute of Chartered Accountants, the most highly respected professional body of accountants in Britain. Yet, if the same man stole a six-pack of beer he would be arrested. If he held up a market with a water pistol and took a hundred dollars, he would go to prison.

There is no truth and no justice in the money system, the political system, or the legal system. I don't think we owe it a duty of truth or justice. I think our duty is to destroy it – not just by "any means necessary", but by "any means possible".

It wasn't "necessary" to burn 80,000 Iraqis to death while they were attempting to retreat under American promises that they would be allowed to withdraw, but it was done.

It wasn't "necessary" for the Americans to burn 1 million Japanese to death while they were trying to surrender for a year, but it was done.

It wasn't "necessary" for the followers of Nelson Mandela to necklace thousands of helpless, harmless blacks in South Africa, but it was done. So I will let the humanitarians lecture me on morals next week (leave a message).

Aryans regard it as honourable to rob banks and die in a hail of bullets, but we regard it as dishonourable to lie on a loan application. How many times does the system lie to you? Who voted to flood America and Europe with non-whites? No one. But the Jews say we live in freedom. That's a lie. How did the Jews get their power to lie? By borrowing (granting themselves credits while manipulating interest rates in their favour).

Loan default is only a crime if you make false statements on the loan application (such as going to 10 different finance companies and denying that you have other loans). Make sure they can't trace the money, or every loan will become a "substantive offence" in a RICO indictment – another Jewish concoction.

Now, when you racists start getting large anonymous cash donations, just remember, see, I don't know nuthin' about it, see – I pay my debts, and I always tell the truth.

1994

ON DEMOCRACY

Machiavelli said that the Prince will retain the outer form of traditional institutions while changing their inner substance. This applies in particular to a meaningless concoction popularly known as "Democracy".

"Democracy" includes Communism, but does not include any form of "racial discrimination". Since "racial discrimination" was generally practised until about 40 years ago, this means that "Democracy" is only 40 years old.

If you don't believe in "Democracy", you are a criminal (for example, Gottfried Küssel, who got 11 years and served 8 (!) in Austria for advocating the legalization of the Austrian National Socialist Party (with about 25 members), Günther Deckert, who got 9 months and served 5 years (!!) in Germany for INTERPRETING a speech by Fred Leuchter at a meeting attended by perhaps 200 people; or Hans-Jörg Schimanek, who got 15 years (!!!) in Austria for saying that Austria should be part of Germany and that he didn't believe in the gas chambers. (It was partly for protesting Schimanek's conviction in Austria that I got 5 months in absentia in Germany.)

[Note: Deckert appealed the 9 months, but the prosecutors didn't think the sentence was long enough, so they increased it to 3 years (in America this is called "double jeopardy"). Two of the three judges were unsympathetic to the prosecution and thought it was wrong, so they were forcibly retired on the grounds of "ill health", even though at least one of them (I think there were two) announced publicly that he had never felt better in his life! While he was in jail, Deckert wrote a letter to a Jewish journalist and got 4 more years for offending this super-sensitive Jew (is there any other kind)? So that's how he got 9 months and served 5 years.]

I was rereading "The Thoughts of Chairman Mao" the other night, and lo and behold! The "Great Helmsman" talks about "Democracy" on every page. If we believe in "Democracy", does that mean we believe in Chinese Communism? If Chairman Mao ran for President against The Gang of Four, would we be bound by the results? I don't think so.

The fact is, that "Democracy" is a meaningless noise, the definitions of which are switched whenever it suits the liberals [or the Bushnikoprophagists]. For example: Europeans are expelled from their homes in Asia and Africa where they lived for centuries: that's "Democracy". But we can't expel African and Asian immigrants from their homes in Europe, because that's not "Democracy"! We killed millions of Europeans during WWII to "save Democracy", but we can't kill a few (or a few million) scum immigrants, because that's not "Democracy"!

In short, "Democracy" is like God: you're supposed to believe in it, but nobody can tell you what it means, where it is, or how it works, except that it almost never does anything to help you.

Since "Democracy" has no real meaning, and since the various definitions all contradict each other, and since the very concept implies the suicide of the White Race, I think the term should either cease to be used, or a sensible definition should be devised.

My definition is: "Democracy" means the "Self-Determination of Peoples". "Democracy" is not compatible with the abolition of national borders or with racial and national mixing. I do not believe in a "Democracy" in which every racial, national, ethnic, and religious group is a "minority" to be outvoted by everyone else. Nor is it clear why "minorities" should enjoy special privileges (so-called "rights") in a "Democracy". I believe that all nationalism must be rooted primarily in ethnicity, in race.

According to this definition, then, nationalist dictatorships can be "democratic", but internationalist "Democracy" can never be.

I've lived in two dictatorships, and frankly, there's not that much difference. To me, all political systems are the same. If you agree with the government, you feel free. If you don't agree with the government, you find out you're not so free. If anything, dictatorship is better, because it's more honest. There's less propaganda. There's less censorship. In many ways, there's more freedom. For example:

In Spain and Portugal under Franco and Salazar, you could go anywhere in the country at any time of the day or night, even with a woman, and you felt safe.

Nothing like that in our "Democracies".

[Note: The same thing is true in many Moslem countries. Cairo is one of the biggest cities in the world, but a woman can walk home alone at night, even at 2 in the morning, and feel safe, because rapists are shot or beheaded. Same thing in Tunisia, Morocco, etc. And we're going to teach them about "women's rights"?]

There was only one political party in Portugal, the National Union. But they held elections, with opposition candidates. How much simpler to have 2 parties and control them both (the American system), or 10 parties and criminalize the opposition (the European system).

FOR EXAMPLE:

In Belgium, about 12 years ago, there were 3 anti-immigration parties (the Vlaams Blok, le Front National and AGIR). Between them, they got 750,000 votes, 20% of the total nationwide. You are FORCED TO VOTE in Belgium; failure to do so is punishable by fine or imprisonment, so the voter turnout is 100%. But a lot of people are drunk, or have a hangover, or don't give a damn, so they simply cast blank ballots. Result: the anti-immigration parties and blank ballots totalled between 50 and 65% of the vote!

Anybody can get on the ballot in Belgium with 500 signatures on a petition; every small town has some oddball character running for local office with 500 signatures – there is NO DIRECT VOTING FOR NATIONAL OFFICE in this wonderful "democracy"; the national *nomenklatura* is "elected" by all the local Party *apparatchiks*. So the government indicted 5 officers of one of the largest anti-immigration parties in the country (the "Front National", a Belgian organization entirely separate from the French "Front National") for supposedly FORGING FOURTEEN of their FIVE HUNDRED SIGNATURES on ONE of their local petitions – after getting SEVEN HUNDRED AND FIFTY THOUSAND VOTES nationwide, together with the other two parties! Possible prison sentence: 5 YEARS IMPRISONMENT. They recently outlawed the largest opposition political party in the country, the Vlaams Blok, claiming the party wasn't "democratic"!

About eight years ago, a Belgian group called REF demanded a referendum on immigration. What could be more democratic than allowing the citizens of a country to vote on how many non-citizens they want? But no, that wasn't "democratic" either.

Since when do non-citizens of a country have more rights than citizens? But no, nothing else would be "democratic"!

Having destroyed practically every anti-immigration party in the country, the local oddballs with their 500 signatures all went back to advocating exactly the same things: "fighting unemployment, protecting the environment, and more rapid integration of immigrants" (oh, and I almost forgot: "Not to fear globalization, which will benefit everyone"), with slogans like "Let's Move Forward – Together!" That these programs all contradicted each other bothered no one.

When Hugo Chávez got elected President of Venezuela, he got 116 out 120 seats; the two parties that had run the country for 40 years simply *went out of existence* – literally. Soon afterwards, I translated a position paper for the Social Democrats (who control political parties in dozens of countries) raising a howl against the election, claiming it wasn't "democratic"!

I've also translated large numbers of confidential documents for the so-called "European Communities", and personally I prefer Communism. Under Communism, somebody is responsible for everything. Stalin signs an order, it's signed "Stalin". Then, when things go wrong, some Commissar gets the blame, and he gets shot. But at least you have the satisfaction of knowing that somebody got shot, and that the next clown probably will be, too. The EEC destroys industries, putting hundreds of thousands of people out of work, and the order ("called a "Guideline" or a "European Directive") is signed simply: "The Commission". There are no names. Nobody knows who that means. Stalin was more honest. If you killed him, the system would change. In the end, he was supposedly poisoned by his doctors, and the system *did* change. The bureaucracy of the EEC resembles everything I've ever read about Communism; it's just more sophisticated (so far). If Stalin was a "nation-killer", then what is the EEC?

In 1958, the opposition candidate for President of Portugal, Humberto Delgado, got too many votes running against incumbent President Américo Tomás, so they changed the Constitution! What could be more "democratic" than that?

The Salazar regime in Portugal (1926-1974) was by all accounts the one of the most repressive dictatorships in 20th century Europe, fighting a 13-year war against Communist guerrillas in 3 African colonies 22 times the size of Portugal (1961-1974). The Communist Party was outlawed and was forbidden to organize. But you could buy Communist books in any student bookstore: complete speeches of Castro, complete works of Stalin, anything you wanted (at least towards the very end). The same was true in Spain. Assuming that the "Democracies" are still at war with the National Socialists (55 years later), can you buy revisionist books in any bookstore, anywhere in the world? Of course not. You can't even buy "The Hoax of the Twentieth Century" at Arthur Butz's own university.

One reason the Portuguese went to war in Africa was because 750,000 Portuguese lived there. They fought for 13 years, in a war they couldn't win no matter how long they fought, and no matter what they did. In the end, the Communist-indoctrinated Army officer class, conscripted out of the universities, got fed up and overthrew the government.

The Americans, by contrast, fought for 9 years in Viet Nam, a country where no Americans ever lived, in a war they could have won in 6 weeks by bombing the dikes and docks in North Viet Nam. This was never done. Instead, the North Vietnamese were notified, in advance, of which targets would be bombed, on which dates, so that they could concentrate their anti-aircraft fire around precisely those targets.

The only intention of the American government in any war is to fight just long enough to get a lot of people killed, and then give everything away to the Communists (or Zionists). Objectively, the duty of the US armed forces in Viet Nam was either to refuse to fight or to overthrow the government and win the war. This was never done either. The US Army doesn't overthrow governments. Why not? Because we live in a "Democracy". Proof that there's more freedom in dictatorships.

In dictatorships, newspapers are subject to pre-publication censorship, or post-publication seizure. The seizures are usually treated as something of a joke, and always result in increased circulation. For example, in Portugal, every newspaper carried a notice saying: "*This edition has been reviewed by the censorship commission*". Dreadful! Shocking!

When Fred Leuchter got arrested, somebody sent me 2 newspaper clippings, one from Seattle, Washington, and one from Huntsville, Alabama. Two newspapers, 2,000 miles apart. The articles were almost word for word the same. Why? Because there are only 2 wire services in America. Dictatorships are more honest.

Both Franco and Salazar enjoyed the many jokes told about them. Salazar in particular had an extremely malicious sense of humour. Portugal had 1 television channel, controlled by the government. Every 15 minutes there was an Omo Detergent commercial which consisted of an obvious (and very cruel) joke directed at the President of Portugal, Américo Tomás (pronounced Too-MAHSH). The commercial consisted of a cartoon of a senile old man wearing a sailor suit, like Donald Duck, hopping up and down and jabbering about how he was going to wash his "little sailor suit" – "*o meu fatinho, o meu fatinho, o meu fatinho, tinho, tinho de marujo*" – in Omo Detergent! Tomás was an 85-year-old naval officer who always wore a spotlessly white dress uniform; he often appeared on television directly after this commercial. You couldn't open a newspaper without seeing him. He was treated as a laughing stock because all he did was dedicate monuments and make speeches; but in fact he was the most powerful man in the country: he had the power to dismiss the Prime Minister, Marcelo Caetano, a much younger and more liberal man who did all the real work (Salazar was alive, but he was in the hospital). This was after 9 years of war (1969-70). Nobody noticed. Nobody thought anything of it.

How much more "Democratic" to have 200 television channels (cable, satellite, etc.), control them all, and react with Stalinist hysteria and repression (five-year prison sentences, loss of civil rights, huge fines, etc.) at the slightest jocular reference to anything. A few years ago, I heard a Portuguese pop singer complaining about censorship under the dictatorship. If they didn't like the lyrics, he couldn't release the record; but he wasn't fined or imprisoned. Hans-Jörg Schimanek should be so lucky. In Spain today, it's against the law to tell jokes about the King!

If you can buy Communist books in anti-Communist dictatorships, but cannot buy revisionist books in a "Democracy"; if you can make jokes about the head of state in a dictatorship, but cannot make jokes about Jews, "gays", blacks, etc. etc., in a "Democracy", then what does that tell us about the horseshit "Democracies" in which we live?

Most dictatorships come to power after periods of national anarchy and chaos, and their only real concern is to maintain order and protect certain vested interests. Most dictators attempt to identify themselves with the traditional patriotic values of the nation. To a traditional dictator, patriotism is enough. They don't care what you do, unless you do something in politics against them. In this sense, there can be very great freedom in a dictatorship.

In a dictatorship, national policy is set by the Head of State. In a "Democracy", everything is for sale on the stock exchange. "Democracy" is government by news media, by advertising. Even if 99% of the population are bitterly opposed to something, their opinions are ignored. The politicians follow their mass media slave masters every time. Whose little country am I? Anyone who has money to buy. The media slave masters don't even use their own money. They don't even have to borrow it. They use your money. For example, do you have an insurance policy or pension fund? All of that money is invested in the stock market. Insurance companies and pension funds are the biggest investors on Wall Street. They are also very big advertisers. Then, somebody representing the pension fund calls up the TV station and says, "We didn't like that program last week. We want more multiracialism. Shape up or we're withdrawing our ads." They use your money to destroy your life. Does that seem "Democratic" to you? You bet your life it's "Democratic".

Dictators can be killed or overthrown; it happens rather frequently. But how can you fight the stock exchange? You could shoot thousands of fund managers, and nothing would change. Nobody is ever responsible for anything.

Nobody ever disappears down a Memory Hole in a traditional dictatorship. Dictators often take a dislike to a certain artist or writer, but they don't pretend he never existed. On the contrary, they use the artist's "degeneracy", etc., to justify their own dictatorship.

Every society has certain moral standards. Even cannibals and head-hunters regulate every aspect of their lives by rigid taboos. A tribesman who refuses to conform is killed or expelled from the tribe.

"Democracy", as imagined by the liberals – a society in which everyone is "Free" to do everything except "Hate", i.e., criticize the liberals and their menagerie of pet freaks – has never existed and never will.

Far from being something very new, "Democracy" is a retrogressive form of government, predating hereditary monarchy. Under a system of elective monarchy (for example, Spain between the 6th and 8th centuries, Denmark up until the 16th century, much of German history, and most of Polish history), the king was elected by the nobles. This system was abandoned because it led to constant foreign invasion and civil war. There was always a noble with a claim to the throne who called in foreign troops to support that claim. In Poland, the result was 700 years of chaos. Far from being the irrational institution that Americans think it is, hereditary monarchy was a tremendous innovation in the art of government.

In modern "Democracies", foreign voters are imported. Party A imports 1 million scum immigrants to vote for Party A, while Party B imports 2 million scum immigrants to vote for Party B. Democracy is gerrymandering on a worldwide scale.

In fascist dictatorships, there are no elections, so there is no need for foreign voters. (The National Socialists held a secret referendum every year instead.) Generally, the economy is run at a surplus; popular support is purchased through extensive investment in public works (hydroelectric plants, public utility companies, steel mills, swamp clearance projects, etc.). Fascist regimes balance the budget while undertaking extensive internal improvements. This seemingly impossible feat does not fit into the standard right-left dichotomy.

The financial success of fascist government is easily explained. Fascist regimes, like all governments, finance most of their activities on the bond markets. But unlike Communist regimes, they do not interfere with the profit motive, and unlike "Democratic" regimes, they do not degenerate into chaos. Instead, they offer the prospect of a government which is strong enough to eliminate waste and pay interest on bond issues.

It's not true that you get uniformity of opinion in dictatorships. What you get is a range of opinion acceptable to the government. For example, you may have the Catholics, conservatives, monarchists, moderate socialists, fascists, etc. It's the same in a "Democracy". You get a range of opinion acceptable to the Jews.

Dictatorships don't try to get inside your mind and change the way in which you think on hundreds of different subjects. In a "Democracy", for example, you are bombarded with "new items" and sob stories designed to change your attitudes towards transsexuals for two weeks, after which transsexuals are totally forgotten and the media become obsessed with something else.

In dictatorships, propaganda and censorship are recognized for what they are. People are extremely sceptical. They don't believe everything they read. They believe very little. In a very general way, there is probably far greater fear of expressing "forbidden thoughts" in a "Democracy" – where "forbidden thoughts" are infinitely numerous and are constantly changing with ephemeral mass media fashion – than in dictatorships, where the only forbidden thought is "being against the government" (and doing something about it, for example, organizing a demonstration).

People are more alert in dictatorships, because they know where the propaganda is coming from: the government. In a "Democracy", you're bombarded with propaganda from so many different angles and in so many disguises that you think it's a "plurality" of opinion. But it's not.

Dictatorships are societies like any other, and the same sorts of people are in positions of influence. As always, you can do anything you want until you interfere with somebody who has more influence than you do. In Spain in 1936, in a democracy, the homosexual poet Federico García Lorca molested the son of a Civil Guard and was taken out and shot.

[Note: Technically, it is, of course, an error to state that Lorca was shot in a "democracy". He was shot 30 days after the outbreak of the war, when the Nationalists overran Granada, where he was living. The reason for the shooting – recognised as a disgrace to Spain and a crime against literature worldwide, even by nationalists – was his homosexual seduction of the son of a Civil Guard.

As ye do, so shall ye get did.

Source: Private information from a resident of Granada, generally conceded to be more or less the truth. García Lorca was not politically committed and was not particularly radical. After all, nobody shot the famous philosopher Unamuno, an open enemy of the nationalists, even after he insulted Millán Astray, the most fanatical of all nationalist generals, in public and to his face.

The philosophers and Greek professors and lyric poets like Unamuno and García Lorca can cogitate and sololoquize and split hairs all they want, but it is obvious that the future belongs to men like Millán Astray, whether we like it or not, and whether we admit it or not.

Our enemies all know this and are putting it into effect on a daily basis.

It is interesting to note that Unamuno supported the Nationalists at first, like the middle classes virtually all over Spain, but, like all intellectuals, was always changing sides. Nothing can be achieved with such people.]

In 1965, under the dictatorship, I asked one of the top officials of the Faculty of Medicine of the University of Cádiz whether I could play the piano. The students told me not to, saying: "Look out, he's a raving queer." [*"Está casado y tiene seis hijos, pero es el maricón más grande de toda Cádiz"*; he was the *rector* or *decano*, I forget which.] I knocked on the door to his office. He said, *"Pase* [come in]". I opened the door. Without a word, he got up, walked around me, shut the door, came back, and started to unbutton my shirt. I told him to stop. He said, *"¿Porqué?"* This was right after class, in the university building, under the so-called "rigidly puritanical Catholic dictatorship".

How could a person like that keep his job for even 5 minutes? Because for every "raving queer", there are 10 secret homosexual sympathizers protecting him. All nationalist societies in history (even primitive tribes) have been anti-homosexual, because homosexuals build a state within a state, like the Jews or Freemasons, and destroy everything which does not suit them personally. This process is now reaching its epitome in the United States. Homosexuality is now taught by law as "normal" in public schools (California), while heterosexuality is progressively criminalized as "Sexual Harassment". In New Mexico, a 13-year-old boy was recently booked for "Sexual Assault" – a criminal felony – for slapping a girl of the same age on the buttocks! He could perform sodomy in the same school, probably even in public, and it would be a "Hate Crime" to criticize him! Interracial rape is no longer punished; black rapists are not even suspended from the basketball team! If homosexuals offend you, you are a "Hate Criminal". If you offend them, you are a "Hate Criminal" again. It can't work any other way. That's the way the liberals want it. Liberals are universal destroyers, like Ghenghis Khan.

In Spain towards the end of the dictatorship, I was stopped by the secret police (in "democracies" we call them "detectives" or "plain-clothes policemen") for failure to carry an identity document and held in a police station for several hours. The police had nothing else to do, so they stood around criticizing the government to me for about an hour. Could a white police detective criticize Affirmative Action to a foreigner in front of witnesses in a police station in New Orleans? It's probably a "Hate Crime" even to ask the question.

You are always free at somebody else's expense. What we call "Democracy" is merely the name that we gave to a dictatorship of our own values when we were confident of them and willing to impose them by force. For example, 30 years ago, homosexual acts were a crime in every state except Illinois; but you could place a racial covenant in the deed to your house, stating that the property could never be re-sold to anyone with African ancestry. Now it's the other way around. Homosexuals are worshipped (their obnoxious behaviour and AIDS notwithstanding), but you're a criminal if you discriminate racially with your own property. You are an object of opprobrium if you discriminate in choosing your own friends.

Are we any freer than we ever were? Of course not. It depends which gang you belong to. One dictatorship has been substituted for another. You can say, "It's my body", and murder your children – that's "Choice" – but you can't say "It's my apartment", "It's my house", "It's my job", or "It's my country". – that's "Discrimination". Yet "Discrimination" is a form of "Choice" (6th definition in the Webster's Unabridged). What's the difference logically?

"Democracy" is dictatorship plus salesmanship. To be effective, propaganda must reverberate from all sides, and must appear to offer the sucker a choice. One egg or two in your malt? Do you want the blue one or the red one? Shall we deliver it today or tomorrow?

Dictatorship says, "You're going to have an egg in your malt because it's good for you, and it's 25 cents extra". It's like truth in advertising.

In a dictatorship, propaganda issues from one central source, and for that very reason is much less effective.

This is why dictatorship is preferable as a system.

Dictatorships justify other dictatorships. It never occurs to our enemies that whatever they do to us today justifies whatever we do to them tomorrow.

Since the victory of the dictatorship of the liberals [or the Bushniks and his hen-house of Jewish neo-cons, for that matter] means the destruction of all values, not to mention civilization, culture, and the White Race, I prefer a nationalist dictatorship of my values to a liberal [or neo-con] dictatorship of theirs.

Our greatest enemy is the delusion that we live in freedom. In fact, what we live in is a dictatorship of the Jews. The more the Jews do to destroy the illusion of freedom, the better. The more persecution of "racists" and "Hoaxoco$t Deniers", the more "Human Rights Tribunals", the better. The Jews don't care about racists, and they don't care how many Turks you set fire to. They only care about the Revisionists, because Revisionists prove that the National Socialists were right about the Jews. That is why you almost never hear about the

Revisionists. Nobody ever heard of Fred Leuchter until they arrested him on his way to a TV station. Nobody ever hears about Revisionists until they go to court. There is more interest in Revisionists today than ever before, even in the mainstream media. The dictatorship of the Jews is backfiring in a big way.

So, the plan is: We use the same tactics which proved so successful for the blacks and homosexuals: calculated obnoxiousness, deliberate provocation, and political extremism for its own sake. This causes the Jews to lose their marbles and resort to increasingly dictatorial tactics. This destroys the value of their own propaganda, which is then seen to issue from a central source. This puts us in the position of being able to accuse them of "Destroying Democracy". Then, we fight a revolution to "Restore Democracy", and set up a dictatorship of our own, called "Democracy". Our dictatorship will have 2 wire services, 2 political parties, and 5 acceptable shades of opinion, represented by major magazines and newspapers, TV, etc., all favourable to us. Control will be exercised financially. Anybody we don't like will be accused of "Not Believing in Democracy" and will be killed. Any time the natives get restless, we start a war to install "Democracy" (as defined by us) someplace else (on the other side of the world). In short, we'll make America the way it used to be when it was a decent country (admittedly, that was a long time ago)!

The Americans will eat it up. You don't need brains when you're dealing with them. *"Whistle while you work, Hitler is a jerk"*. That's their intellectual level. And the best part of it is: it's all been done before. It doesn't pay to be original in politics.

1994–2007

ON GLOBALIZATION

So Why Not?

Having flooded America and Europe with coloured immigrants on the pretext that they would do our "dirty work" for us, the capitalists are now moving all jobs to the non-white world, leaving us to fight over the crumbs.

There is an aspect to this problem which the capitalists have forgotten.

There is only one thing which makes anything cheaper in a foreign country than it is at home, and that is the exchange rate between the two currencies. For example, at 200 yen to the dollar, Japanese cars would be cheap, but at 1 yen to the dollar, they would be ridiculously expensive.

There are two types of exchange rates: free rates (preferred by the capitalist democracies) and fixed rates (preferred by all nationalist economies and dictatorships). Free rates also exist under dictatorships, but are called "black market rates".

Prices are low in the non-white world because their currencies are worthless. Their currencies are worthless because they have abandoned fixed exchange rates. They have abandoned fixed exchange rates because of a deal with the Western capitalists.

In the 1950s, there were 8 Mexican pesos to the dollar. Then, due to high inflation, Mexico wasn't cheap any more. So, they devalued to 12 pesos to the dollar. This was under the old system of fixed rates, which was later abandoned. Then in 1982, due to mismanagement of their oil revenues and other problems, there was a financial panic and crash in which the peso fell to 1000 to the dollar with violent fluctuations. Of course, Mexican officials all had bank accounts in the United States.

At that time, it was theoretically possible (using dollars) to buy very valuable assets in Mexico for a fraction of their real value. This was offset by the risk that the peso might continue to fall to 2000 or even lower, and that any profit in pesos would be blocked by exchange controls or otherwise confiscated or nationalized. [It eventually fell to 12,000 to the dollar, so they introduced a new currency, the "New Peso".]

By some curious coincidence, this is exactly the manner in which the Soviet Union was industrialized in the 1930s, and this is exactly the manner in which Jews and other foreign capitalists bought control of Germany during the inflation of the 1920s. In fact, come to think of it, this is the way in which the Mexican railroads and oil industries were built and developed in the first place (under Porfirio Díaz, overthrown in 1911).

In other words, it was a political deal in which the foreign capitalists got caught in their own trap and lost their money.

At the same time, these countries are taking out hard currency loans to pay for Western infrastructures which would never be sold to them for local currency. This adds to the sum total of bad debt in the world. China, for example, is acquiring total nuclear technology from France, and not in Chinese play money either. Oh well, let them blow each other up.

This is also the reason for the destruction of South Africa. A period of chaos will drive the prices down and destroy the exchange rate, after which the niggers can be bought off (value of Rand in 1973: US$ 1.15; value of Rand today: 16 US cents at most, sometimes half that. Value of Rhodesian dollar in 1973: US$ 2.00; value of "Zimbabwean" dollar today: 2 or 3 US cents). [2007 update: Worthless. According to a recent news item, the government decided to print trillions of dollars worth of worthless new currency, but could not even afford to pay for the paper!]

What would happen if America used the same methods? I think it would go something like this:

Let us assume that when the revolution comes, our industrial plant is obsolete, and that most Americans are unemployed. Let us assume that there are 200 yen to the dollar.

Presto! We introduce fixed exchange rates, with the death penalty for all black marketeers.

We devalue the dollar to 1 yen. This makes Japanese products ridiculously expensive. Capitalists with yen make huge speculative profits (since the yen is now worth 200 times as much), so we shoot all the capitalists (that's what the Chinese would do, so why not?)

Then, at 1 yen to the dollar, America is so absurdly cheap from the Japanese point of view that the Japs build thousands of new factories in America. At the same time, we contract huge debts that we don't intend to pay.

Then we nationalize all foreign investment. We now have all new industrial plant at no cost to us, built by the Japanese. Then we devalue again and shoot the Jews; not because we are "anti-Semitic", but for "economic wrecking" and "social parasitism". That's what the Chinese would do, so why not?

1992–2001

ON IMMIGRATION

Two Can Play That Game

There is only one issue: White Race survival.

But while we're waiting for the Thought Police (with a pump .12 gauge and plenty of ammo), how about another round of intellectual masturbation on philosophical topics?

In classical philosophy, it was considered axiomatic that identical causes have identical effects.

Of course, today the Jews have changed all that, and the effect is always the same, absolutely regardless of the cause. For example:

a) France had colonies in North Africa; France is full of Arabs.

b) Belgium never had any colonies in North Africa; Belgium is full of Arabs.

c) Britain had African colonies; Britain is full of blacks.

d) Germany lost all its colonies in 1919; Germany is full of blacks.

e) America fought in Viet Nam; America is full of Vietnamese.

f) Germany never had anything to do with Vietnam; Germany is full of Vietnamese.

g) America is a "nation of immigrants", so we are packed out with scum; nations that were never "nations of immigrants", like Italy and Ireland, are packed out with scum nevertheless.

And so on, *mutatis mutandis*. There are probably more Mozambicans in Germany than there are in Portugal, although Mozambique was a Portuguese colony. Why? Because there's more welfare in Germany than there is in Portugal.

This is called "*manipulating the logical argument to get what you want regardless of the factual situation*", a practice followed by the Jews at all times and under all circumstances.

Well, two can play that game. For every action, there is an equal and opposite reaction.

So how about this?

a) Wetbacks without amnesty are here illegally, and are criminals; they can get out.

b) Wetbacks with amnesty are here legally, and have been rewarded for breaking the law; they can get out, too.

c) European blacks came over voluntarily (to sponge off us);

they can get out.

d) American blacks came over involuntarily, as slaves, and are sponging off us, too; they can get out, too.

Why not? What's the difference logically?

Same for European Arabs (with the possible exception of a few *"harki"*, loyal Algerians who came to France to avoid getting their throats cut by the FLN, while hundreds of thousands of others like them were abandoned); but that's a different story. There were 14,000 harki; that doesn't account for two million Arabs in France, 500,000 in Belgium (which never had anything to do with the war in Algeria, not to mention Britain, and every other country in Europe, where they are nothing but a nuisance, etc. etc.).

The White Race is the product of millions of years of evolution. OK. You don't believe in evolution; the same argument applies nonetheless. If the White Race is the product of Divine Creation, that makes it even more precious, rather than less.

Slavery, segregation, and apartheid were all justified on Biblical grounds, and quite correctly so, too; now the Christians tell us WE can't be racists, but the Zionists CAN be. The fact remains that the Bible does not advocate racial mixing.

The White Race has survived thousands of years of authoritarianism. It will not survive 250 years of democracy. This makes *"democracy"* the worst form of government, bar none.

Not that I am not a believer in authoritarianism on principle. On the contrary, I think the U.S. Constitution is the greatest purely political document in history. But I want it the way it was originally written and intended.

For example:

a) If the Confederate states were not entitled to leave the Union under the 10th Amendment, they were still in the Union when the 1861-65 Secession War ended. The 13th, 14th, 15th Amendments required the ratification of 27 states, which they never received. These amendments were never legally ratified, and have no binding force. Therefore, blacks are not citizens and cannot vote. All politicians elected with their votes are in office illegally; all legislation passed by those politicians is null and void. This includes the Jewish-sponsored immigration bills that are turning American into a Third World country. This includes all the obviously unconstitutional Supreme Court decisions which are turning America into a garbage dump.

[Note: The 1861-65 conflict was not a *"civil war"* as that term is defined in international law; the term *"civil war"* was, and is, a Northern propaganda term intended to justify Lincoln's illegal invasion of the first seven seceding states which in fact caused the war, including the secession of four more states. As for *"freeing the slaves"*, slavery was never abolished in the North until after Lincoln was killed, and even then it was done illegally. Lincoln was a pathological liar just like F.D.R., Reagan, Clinton, and the Two Bushniks.

For a display of the mental contortions indulged in by Northern imperialists to avoid admitting that the 1861-65 conflict was a "war of secession" and that Northern actions were illegal, see *Wheaton's Elements of International Law*, 1866 Edition, by George Grafton Wilson, with notes by Richard Henry Dana, a Northern fanatic.

For example: War was never declared against the Confederacy, and the Confederacy never surrendered, because the Lincoln government refused to acknowledge its existence!

"The United States could recognize no authority, either of a State or of confederated States, capable even of making a surrender. It would deal only with each army before it, and accept its separate surrender to the commander of the Union army opposed to it, as a military fact. The surrender of all the rebel armies left the confederacy [no capitalization in the original] *simply to collapse. Neither its existence nor its disappearance was noticed legally by the United States"* (p. 70-72, note by Richard Henry Dana).

This is like discharging a shotgun at a ghost while proclaiming loudly that one does not believe in spirits. It was also a violation of the Constitutional provision that only Congress can declare war. All the seceding states had ratified the Constitution by State resolutions expressly reserving the right to secede under the plain language of the 10th Amendment. There is nothing in the Constitution prohibiting secession, even today. It is purely a question of brute force, of naked political power. In fact – *in practice* – the Constitution is not worth the paper it is written on.

As for the slaves, the defeat of the South was a disaster for the blacks, whether they admit or not. Reagan was one of the worst Presidents in American history, because it was he who first began the practice of amnesty for illegal immigrants. One might as well put the country up for auction to the *lowest* bidder.

As for Bush, it would have been better if Gore had been allowed to steal the election, because more people hated him. Which is better, to eat shit and know it's shit, or eat shit and think it's ice cream? I think the first is better, because you'll eat less of it, plus you might kill the ice cream vendor who sold it to you. Hope springs eternal in the human "beast".]

b) Contrariwise: If the Confederate states WERE entitled to leave the Union under the 10th Amendment, the same reasoning applies, and the same consequences follow nonetheless. The 13th, 14th, 15th Amendments required the ratification of 27 states, which they never received. These amendments were never legally ratified, and have no binding force. Therefore, blacks are STILL not citizens and STILL cannot vote. All politicians elected with their votes are in office illegally; all legislation passed by those politicians is STILL null and void. This includes the Jewish-sponsored immigration bills that are turning American into a Third World country. This includes all the obviously unconstitutional Supreme Court decisions which are turning America into a garbage dump.

Slavery was forced on the United States of America before the U.S.A. became an independent country. The Commonwealth of Virginia attempted to abolish slavery in 1750 and was prohibited by the British Crown from doing so. One of the first acts of the newly independent United States was to abolish the international slave trade, becoming effective in 1807.

So if the niggers don't like it here, they can direct their complaints to the Queen of England. She's a nigger-lover, and what's more she's rich, so let her pay.

Which brings us to Free Trade. Some people are against Free Trade, but I'm for it. I think we need it (for about five minutes). Why? Because Free Trade destroys all the pretexts trotted out by Jews to justify unrestricted coloured immigration since 1965 (accompanied, of course, by the abortion of 40 million mostly white children in the US at the same time; what about *their "better life"*?).

For fifty years, we have been told that the *"down-trodden masses"* [to quote the words of Zionist kike Emma Lazarus – look at the way THEY treat people!] of Mexico, Africa, Asia, and the Pacific Islands are flooding into the United States to seek a "better life".

Well, capitalism certainly does produce a "better life" if material things are the sole criterion.

So I say: If China is good enough for the capitalists to invest in, then it is good enough for the Chinese to live there, in the "plenty" that capitalism created for them (assuming that such "plenty" really exists; if it does not, the same principle applies nonetheless).

If Viet Nam is to be the "New Frontier of Capitalism" (according to National Geographic Magazine), then it is good enough for the Vietnamese to live there. Same for all other countries (except for qualified immigrants the way it used to be).

All these countries have entered into highly disadvantageous (to them) financial agreements with Western capitalists. In some cases, Western investors will have recovered 100% of their capital in as little as 4 years. All this investment will be nationalized – sooner or later. Poetic justice.

So we tell them: OK, we invested x-zillion dollars modernizing your countries, you can have it. You can nationalize it. It's yours. We won't send in the Marines the way we did in Vera Cruz, Mexico, in 1914 and 1927, etc. But there's a catch. You gotta take back your people. Otherwise, *swim, baby, swim.*

After all, since the world is round, if you keep on going in any one direction, sooner or later you end up in the same place. That's how America got discovered in the first place. Or have we forgotten?

The wetbacks keep bitching about the *"frontera falsa"*, the "phony border". So where, pray tell, is the *"frontera auténtica"*, the real border? It doesn't correspond to the old pre-Mexican War border, or what the hell are wetbacks doing in places like Georgia and Vermont?

I say: It corresponds to the three-mile limit off the Atlantic Coast (or the North Pole, for all I care; how about the South Pole? Let them keep swimming until they get there).

That's where the *"frontera auténtica"* is. Let's see whether this *"aquatic life form"* adapts to a marine environment.

Same thing for the Jews, who have been saying *"next year in Jerusalem"* for 2,000 years, but who refuse to go there. OK. Let them negotiate with the Arabs on the swim back.

We weren't packed out with illegal refugees in the 1950s, and nobody accused of us being "Nazis" then. So what's happened since?

It's a Jewish verbal quibble, a semantic trick. Anybody who holds what used to be the beliefs of probably 99% of the entire White Race is a "Nazi". (What about the Zio-Nazis?)

Well, I've got a little verbal quibble of my own. Amerigo Vespucci had nothing to do with the 1504 voyage which resulted in the discovery of North America. His claim to have done so is apocryphal (like Himmler's "Secret Speech"). The continent is misnamed.

So we rename the country: The United States of Aryanland. Anybody who isn't an Aryan can get out. Who decides who's an Ayran? We do.

Nobody ever gave us any authority to do this, but nobody ever gave the Jews any authority either (they bought their "authority" on the stock exchange, by manipulating interest rates, borrowing money, and buying up the mass media), so what's the difference?

ADDENDUM: On second thought, skip the "We" and make it "I". If *"democracy"* is a system in which *"minorities"* enjoy special status, and totalitarian dictatorship is government by a minority of one, then totalitarian dictatorship is the perfect form of *"democracy"*. Just read Chairman Mao's *Little Red Book* (or the speeches of Fidel Castro, for that matter).

It's no more absurd than anything else (for example, a mass-media-based "anti-racist" dictatorship of fanatically "racist" Zionist Jews). *So why not?*

1996–2002

ON MULTICULTURALISM

I believe that the environmentalists and multiculturalists are correct in blaming the problems of the world on the white man's interference with the cultural values of the non-white races.

Unlike the multiculturalists, however, I believe in applying multiculturalist arguments literally.

After a century of receiving our charity, the non-white races are now multiplying by the billions, and are immigrating to white countries, where they demand more charity. Multiculturalists insist that we should take them in, but deny that we have anything superior to offer them. Actually, their culture is as good as ours!

If that is so, surely they cannot object if their culture is what we give them. For example:

The Aztec war god, Huitzilopochtli, was fed with the hearts of prisoners, after which the bodies were devoured in a cannibal orgy. Equipped with an export religion to paralyze the intended victims ("Huitzilopochtli is a God of Love", "Aztecs are God's Chosen People", etc.), this religion might have real possibilities (i.e., the bodies could be thrown off the Lincoln Memorial and devoured in front of the Hoaxoco$t Museum).

The Cocoma Indians of Peru ate their dead and dissolved the bones in fermented drink on the grounds that it was "better to be inside a friend than be swallowed up in the cold Earth".

This practice, known as "funeral cannibalism", was once exceedingly common, prevailing throughout Africa, Australia, the South Seas, and South America. The products of putrefaction were licked up as they ran down off the body; the Australian Aborigines smoke-dried their dead, consuming all body parts rendered liquid by the heat.

The beauty of this practice is that it incalculably multiplied the death rate through the spread of contagious disease. This death rate was again doubled by the fact that primitive peoples had, until very recently, no concept of natural death. All death not due to violence was attributed to witchcraft and avenged by murder.

Presumably, this is another value of great relevance and diversity (i.e., the bodies could be allowed to rot for months, and the multiculturalists could eat them).

In India, children were thrown into the Ganges, while the crocodiles who ate them were worshipped. The shortage of crocodiles in California, Canada, Britain, and Europe offers some difficulty, but presumably some suitable substitute could be devised.

Infibulation is another custom of great multicultural richness and relevance. This is the attaching of a ring or clasp to the sexual organs to prevent sexual intercourse. In Africa, this consists of stitching together the labia majora of girls at the age of four or five. (For rap singers and Nelson Mandela, please enrich other end.)

Care for the sick and elderly is a well-known value of primitive peoples. The Eskimos starved their aged and sick; the Chukchi of Siberia stoned or strangled them; some Indian tribes fed them to tigers; the Battas of Sumatra ate them. Just think of the savings in Social Security!

Overpopulation and world hunger are problems created by the white man. The Niam-Niam, Monbuttu, and Maori carried on wars to obtain human flesh; human body parts were exposed for sale in markets; corpses of relatives were sold for food. African and Polynesian cannibals ate their own children; the Tasmanians, when hungry, considered the birth of a child simply the opportunity for a square meal. Fiji chiefs ate their own friends and relatives. Just think of the money saved on Food Stamps!

There are no fraudulent bankruptcies among primitive peoples. The Battas ate their criminals, while some African tribes ate their debtors. Robert Maxwell alone would feed a multitude (smoke-dried).

Homeopathic methods of healing are of great multicultural relevance as well. The Tongans amputated finger joints to allow the escape of evil spirits which brought disease into the body; diseased children were thus mutilated. The Luritcha Aborigines cured sick children by feeding them on younger, healthier, children.

Love of children and large families is another well-known multicultural characteristic. Africans baited lion traps with their own children; South Americans, such as the Moxos, abandoned or killed them without reason. According to Charles Darwin, a Fuegian dashed his child's brains out for simply upsetting a basket of fish. An Australian aborigine, seeing his infant sick, killed, roasted, and ate him.

Personal adornment (no animal testing, please!) is one of the many fields in which non-white cultural values might well be imitated. The Hottentots and Bushmen removed one testicle; the Gallas amputated the nipples of boys; the Australian Aborigines cut open and left exposed the whole length of the urethral canal of the penis. Just the thing for Bill Clinton!

The Botocudos inserted disks of wood into the lower lip. Mangaja women pierced the upper lip and introduced small metal shields or rings. Mittu women thrust wooden pegs through the lips. In other tribes, sticks of rock crystal were pushed through, which jingled together as the wearer talked. Senegalese women increased the thickness of the upper lip by pricking until it was permanently swollen. This presumably renders them irresistible if you can tell the difference.

In Indo-China, the Mois of Annam, the Penangs of Cambodia, and the Dyaks of Borneo extended their ear lobes by the insertion of wooden disks and metal rings and weights until they sometimes reached the shoulder. African and Asian earrings sometimes weighed half a pound. The natives of the Zambesi distended the perforation in the lobe of the ear until the fist could pass through it. The Monbuttos carried rolls of leaves, leather, or cigarettes in their ears. The Papuans, the natives of the New Hebrides, and most Melanesian peoples carried all sorts of things in their ears.

The New Caledonians used their ears as pipe racks. The Berawana of Borneo wore ear plugs 3 and ¾ inches in diameter. A stone Masai ear plug in the British Museum measures 4 and ½ inches in diameter and weighs 2 lbs 14 oz. With the miniaturization of portable radios, this will leave the hands free to mug people.

In New Zealand, earrings were decorated with the teeth of enemies; among the Masai, the lobes were stretched so as to be capable of meeting above the head. The multiculturalists will look simply smashing with their ears in a knot.

In New Guinea, pieces of bone or flowers were thrust through the septum of the nose, a mutilation also practised by New Zealanders, Australians, New Caledonians, and other Polynesians. The African Bagas and Bongos wore metal rings and buckles in their noses. The Aleutian Islanders wore cords, bits of metal or amber in their noses. Unmarried Ababde girls wore no rings in their noses (since most American blacks are illegitimate, this custom is of little relevance).

The Aleutian and Kurile Islanders bored holes in their cheeks and inserted seal whiskers. The Guaranis of Venezuela inserted feathers in the same manner. Thus marked for identification, the multiculturalists can be hunted down and used for food. Why not?

The Hindus burnt all widows alive; the Rajputs killed most of their girls by drowning them in milk; alternatively, the mother's breast was smeared with opium or the juice of a poisonous plant. Another common method was to cause suffocation by covering the child's mouth with cow dung. The Tuski, Ahts, Western Eskimos, and Botocudos killed their infants without distinction of sex. Just think of the savings on Aid to Families with Dependent Children!

Thus it is seen that a true application of multiculturalist values is the "Final Solution" to all the world's environmental, social, financial, and racial problems.

[Source of all information: *1911 Encyclopaedia Britannica*.]

1992–2001

ON SLAVERY

The reason why liberals are called "liberals" is because they want to liberalize everything (when it suits the liberals). Everybody should be free to do anything; everything should be free to everybody (when it suits the liberals; when it doesn't, that is quite a different story). For example:

a) Women die during illegal abortions; abortion should be legalized to ensure proper surgical techniques;

b) Junkies poison themselves with drugs; drugs should be legalized to ensure a clean supply;

c) Prostitutes spread disease and are exploited by pimps; prostitution should be legalized and regulated;

d) Illegal gambling is dishonest because the casinos have to bribe the police; gambling should be legalized to collect tax revenues and to ensure fair play.

Personally, I have a great fondness for this sort of reasoning. For example:

a) Revisionist, racist, and "hate literature" should be legalized in all countries to ensure scrupulous accuracy of content;

b) Racial separation should be legalized and regulated to avoid violent reprisals by dispossessed whites;

c) Burning refugee centres should be legalized and regulated to ensure proper ignition of the various flammable liquids involved and to avoid endangering adjacent properties housing innocent people;

d) The sale of white children for adoption should be legalized and regulated to prevent white people who love children, but can't have any, from importing coloured scum from the Indian sub-continent. Most people who have abortions are egotistical and materialistic. If they could sell their offspring for $25,000 each – probably the average market value for a healthy white child – they would produce one a year. Poo on morals, let's get the white birth rate up! (Of course, this means that the killing of sex perverts who might want to adopt them must also be legalized and regulated.)

e) The lynching of race-mixers, and pervert "rights" activists should be regulated to avoid accidental infection of innocent bystanders with AIDS;

f) The assassination of Federal agents, abortionists, "Fair Housing" spies, etc. should be legalized to avoid shooting next door neighbours by mistake, etc. etc.

Do I advocate murder? Of course not. Murder is illegal. Look at Waco, Texas. If you did that, it would be murder, but the Feds did it, so it's not.

The same reasoning can be applied to slavery and the slave trade. It can easily be shown that the worst features of the trade were caused precisely by its abolition and subsequent illegality. Where it was legal and regulated (such as in the southern states of North America), it was practised with great humanity. Where it has been abolished, it was (and is, since it has now been revived) practised with great cruelty.

The white Christian slave holders of North America were the most humane slave holders the world has ever seen. But their profits were almost nil (about 4% per year on average and 15% per year in exceptional cases; most slave plantations were lucky to break even). All the money made in slavery was made in the Northern shipping trade, and reinvested in Northern industry, in the factory system (yielding about 25% per year on average).

In Liverpool harbour in 1807, there were 740 ships, 25% of total Liverpool-registered shipping, engaged in the transport of 200,000 slaves per year. All these ships were owned either by Jews or by Puritanical Northern Protestants – the same people who later turned their energies to abolitionism, socialism, women's rights, and Prohibition. As soon as they were in a position to help the Negro (after the so-called Civil War or War Between the States), the Negro was forgotten, and other problems were discovered (or invented). That is the psychology of the Northern liberal.

Slaving was always the most dangerous of all shipping trades, because of the danger of fever and epidemics. That's why it had to be the most profitable. It's the logic of the free market. But as long as the trade was legal, slavers could be certain of reaching their destination. They had no incentive to overcrowd. In fact, they were likely to do the opposite, to keep the death rate down.

With the abolition of the slave trade under international law, ship owners had to expect that perhaps only one ship in four would get through.

The slave trade was abolished through international treaties giving the British navy the right to "stop and visit" (search) the ships of other maritime nations on the open sea. All ships of a signatory nationality found to be in violation of the treaty were confiscated as "fair prize" by the British warships, and sold at auction at an "Admiralty Prize Court" in London. The proceeds were split half to the British Crown, and half to the officers of the vessel responsible for the capture.

This meant that British Navy officers were given a powerful financial incentive to permit the loading of illegal slaves, and then seize the ship. Standard practice was to lie in wait off the coast of West Africa and begin pursuit on the open sea.

A slave ship, once sighted by the British, might be under pursuit for as much as entire day or more, sometimes escaping in fog and coming under pursuit again days later. Captained and crewed by criminals, carrying an illegal cargo, and in desperate need to lighten the ship, an inferior vessel had a powerful incentive to "do the right thing" by throwing the slaves overboard.

This saved the British the trouble of repatriating the blacks to Africa, or even transporting them to the nearest land. How very convenient.

For this very reason, many prestigious American diplomats (for example, Secretary of State Henry Clay and Ambassador to France Lewis Cass) opposed ratification of these treaties. They foresaw that interference with the American shipping trade would not stop the trade, but would simply aggravate the problem (i.e., the cargo would be fed to the sharks, the ships confiscated, and the crews imprisoned).

An anti-slavery treaty with Brazil, signed in 1827, had no effect whatsoever on the importation of slaves, who continued to be imported at the rate of 50,000 per year).

Historically, slavery arises as an alternative to the killing of prisoners of war, and, as such, is a positive good. The Romans are thought to have owned 16 million slaves. In primitive societies, slavery is even an essential stage in the progress of civilization. It enables a tribe of predatory hunter-gatherers to settle down to a life of agriculture. Of course, where the enslavement of one's own race (for example, Africans by Africans) may be beneficial, the enslavement of Africans by whites or Arabs leads to race mixing and race suicide. It follows that the enslavement of blacks by whites must be condemned.

All religions invented by, or copied from, Jews (including Christianity, but particularly Islam) preach the legality of slavery (for example Exodus 21:20 or Leviticus 25:44), but advocate equality with freed slaves. The Arabs, who 2,000 years ago were a Semitic race of whites, are today a Semitic race of mongrels, incapable of attaining their former levels of civilization, at one time among the highest in the world.

Most American blacks are thought to have been Yorubas enslaved by the Dahomeys, who would otherwise have killed or eaten them. Since the enslavement of blacks by blacks can be beneficial, but since the enslavement of blacks by whites is a crime (not against the blacks, but against future generations of whites), it follows that we must make amends.

In fact, we have already made amends: we destroyed slavery in the only way in which it could be destroyed: through the occupation of the entire coastline of Africa and all the principal slaving centres (such as Bagirmi in the Sudan, a thriving centre for the Arab trade in eunuchs) by Europeans. This was called "Colonialism".

Since colonialism is a now a thing of the past, and since the conditions which create slavery persist, slavery has now returned, in a variety of forms. There is an Anti-Slavery Society in London; there is an Anti-Slavery Commission in the U.N.

Since it has returned, according to the logic of the liberals, it should be legalized and regulated. The only problem is that the hundreds of millions of Africans who could otherwise be used for this purpose are too exhausted by cholera, typhoid, AIDS, and tribal massacres to do any useful work for their racial brethren. At the same time, we have tens of millions of American blacks who are deprived by our welfare system of the satisfaction of productive labour.

To sum up, slavery should be re-legalized and regulated to ensure the collection of tax revenues and proper conditions (with, of course, the trade flowing in the opposite direction, since slavery is no longer required in North America).

Anything can be done in politics, provided that suitable euphemisms be invented. *What is "Democracy" but an ideology to be imposed by force, like "Fascism"? What is the "New World Order" but a plot to enslave everyone?* What are Fair Housing, Equal Opportunity, and Affirmative Action but plots of enslavement?

There is therefore no reason why American blacks cannot be re-enslaved and re-sold to their former black masters in Africa, provided that suitable euphemisms consisting of Federal-style gobbledygook be devised.

I suggest "AFRICAN INDUSTRIAL DEVELOPMENT SERVICE – OVERSEAS UNIT TRANSFER"? (A.I.D.S.-O.U.T.) (unit = 1 nigger).

With a bit of imagination, and some luck, this could easily become "Underwater Unit Transfer" i.e., we ensure the ships for large sums with Jewish-owned banks and insurance companies, then sink them (the Jews go along as financial advisors.)

Insurance companies being what they are, however, probably 75% of all our claims will never be paid, whether justified or not. We'll have to sink the lot just to collect on any of them. Oh well.

All we have to do now is borrow the money to pay the premiums.

[Principal source of historical information: *1911 Encyclopaedia Britannica.*]

* * *

In my view, only a person with a proper understanding of Southern history can understand the hypocrisy, brutality and greed of the Northern capitalist mentality which now has now taken over and destroyed the entire country, including the South, with its emphasis on expediency, "fun", selfishness, short-term profit and practicality over principle.

The Confederates were the last honest Americans. We will not see their like again.

With respect.

The grey riders are gone, and yet they remain,
Asleep in our soil and alive in our veins.
Untouched by fire, untouched by frost,
They whisper within us: our cause is not lost
                                         – Unknown

* * *

Recommended website: http://www.johnbellhood.org.

Gallant website in defence of a gallant Southern gentleman and courageous general. Very scholarly; one of the best I've seen.

* * *

I have been accused by several idiots in the discussion groups of "advocating the reintroduction of slavery".

Of course, there is no need for me to "advocate" any such thing, since slavery has already been reintroduced, and exists now. There are tens of millions of slaves in the world, today, many of whom can be purchased for almost nothing.

The point is: Should this state of affairs – this inescapable fact of life – be recognized, legalized and regulated, according to the principles of the liberals?

It could also be legalized and regulated (in many cases) according to the principles of the Objectivists, Libertarians and Free Traders, as long as there was a "contract" of some sort (coolies, peons, sharecroppers, etc., not to mention the age-old practice of selling oneself into slavery to pay one's debts, quite a relevant idea at present).

Who cares if they don't read the fine print?

That's the "Free Market"!

Actually, this is already being done as a freak sideshow to the Great Libertarian Abortion Debate – if we have a "right" to kill a foetus in the womb, do we also have the "right" to kill or abandon our children after birth? After all, logically, it's more or less the same thing. Regardless of whether or not we have a "right" to kill or abandon them, do we have the "right" to enslave them? After all, we made them, therefore they are "ours". Why not?

One should never underestimate the irrationality and inhumanity of the Libertarian and Objectivist movements.

I could never have imagined the following "rational arguments" even in my wildest moments as a satirist.

Examples:

The foetus is an "aggressor", the foetus is a "trespasser", etc. etc. etc.

The foetus is guilty of the "initiation of physical force" [!] by "occupying your property" [!], etc. etc. etc. therefore it may be "evicted" [!] or "expelled" [!], etc. etc. etc.

One of the foremost proponents of this line of "rational argument" is the "libertarian" Murray Rothbard, a Jew so ugly he makes an ant-eater look like Brad Pitt.

This is Talmudism.

What is slavery compared to this?

1992–2008

ON STALIN

Written in response to an anti-Semite who praised Stalin for shooting a few Jewish commissars starting in 1947 [actually 1933, since most of them were always Jewish to start with].

"Thank you, dear Stalin, for shooting our parents!"

...Let us then adopt Stalin as our model. If we really want to solve our racial problems, our model must then be, not Hitler, who was a babe in the woods when it came to deportations, mass killings, and lying, but Stalin, the past master of all time. What a pity that it took the Man of Steel so long to get around to killing the right people.

— what a pity to have forgotten to shoot his Jewish brother-in-law, Lazar Kaganovich (responsible for seven million deaths in the Ukraine), who lived to be 100 years old;

— what a pity to have built the White Sea Canal with the forced labour of 300,000 Aryans, instead of Jews;

— what a pity to have sent tens of millions of Aryans to labour camps in the Arctic, instead of Jews;

— what a pity to have liquidated "the Kulaks as a class" instead of "the Jews as a race";

– what a pity to have shot 15,000 Polish officers (actually, half of them were loaded onto barges and drowned in the White Sea), instead of 15,000 Jews, etc.;

– what a pity to have killed thirty to sixty million Aryans instead of thirty to sixty million Jews (there must be at least sixty million Jews in the world, if not even more);

– but thank you *"ever so much"* for killing Trotsky with an ice axe (*"one Jew, one ice pick"*), not to mention a few dozen Jewish commissars during the Purge Trials of the 1930s.

After all, a journey of a thousand miles begins with a single step!

Let us then adopt Stalin as our model. Let us adopt the Communist code of morals (which is also the code of the Jews and the Christians), and state openly that the "End Justifies the Means".

[Note: The principle that *"the end justifies the means"* is of Jesuit origin, and is expressed as *"Quum finis est licitus etiam media sunt licita"* in the *Medulla theologiae moralis* by Father Hermann Busenbaum, published in 1645, which went through two hundred editions in little over a century. As a "religion of love" that burnt people alive for 1500 years, Christianity can hardly lay claim to any other basic principle.]

For example:

– if we had taken ten million Africans and drowned them (instead of enslaving them like their African and Arab brethren), we would have been doing the world a favour;

– if we had castrated them for sale as harem guards, like the Arabs (instead of encouraging them to breed like rats so we could sell their children), we would have been doing the world a favour;

– if we had taken 80,000 Mexican wetbacks and burned them alive in the California desert (instead of 80,000 Iraqi soldiers on the other side of the world) [Highway of Death], we would have been doing the world a favour (after all, the Mexicans are *"invading"* us, why shouldn't such *"aggression"* be "punished"? What's the difference logically?);

– if we had taken 300,000 Jewish cultural anthropologists, bankers, financial consultants, investment advisors, lawyers, psychoanalysts, psychiatrists, and psychologists, and burned them alive in Beverly Hills (instead of 300,000 white women and children, helpless refugees, at Dresden, on Stalin's orders via Churchill), we would have been doing the world a favour.

If Stalin can murder 20 or 30 million Russians and be a hero to the President of the United States of America; if Mao Tse Dung can murder 60 million Chinese and be a hero to virtually all Ivy League college students during the war in Viet Nam; if we can murder 50 million of our own children through abortion since 1973, why can't we solve our racial problems in the same way? Why should gassing the Jews be a crime? What's the difference logically?

Under Stalin, the Soviet Constitution guaranteed freedom of speech, freedom of the press, and the right of the republics to secede from the Soviet Union. Of the thirty-two men who wrote this document, thirty were shot by Stalin; yet it was never repudiated. On the contrary, it was quoted by Franklin D. Roosevelt to prove that Soviet Russia was a *"Western-style Democracy"*. If F.D.R. was insane enough to butcher half the world and give the other half to Stalin, why shouldn't Stalin accept it in the spirit in which it was given?

Stalin was a Georgian, a race famous for its implacable vindictiveness. A Georgian will wait twenty years to get revenge for anything. Stalin himself said, *"To lay one's plans carefully, to wreak an implacable vengeance, and then to go to sleep, there is nothing sweeter in the world"*.

One of Stalin's associates said, *"To work with Stalin for thirty years, and still not to know what he is thinking; that is terrible."* I think this is an admirable quality; that is the spirit we need.

What a thrill it would be to put thousands of Federal agents and officials on trial in Washington in a Stalin-like show trial and hear them snivel, *"I have betrayed my race; I am scum deserving only to be shot"*, and to see them applaud frantically when death sentences were handed down upon them.

What a thrill it would be to do the same to the *"Politically Correct"* commissars of American cultural and political life.

That would be Stalinist procedure. That is *"Democratic"*. That is therefore acceptable in the United States of America. National Socialist procedures are not acceptable.

The lessons of history are clear. If you steal, steal big. If you kill, kill big. If you lie, lie big. It is in this last respect that Hitler proves the most deficient. Hitler appears to have been a very poor liar. He seems to have had an almost incurable predilection for the truth; a fatal weakness in 20th century politics.

Look at the British. They put up a monument to Butcher Harris, who killed a million civilians on purpose, and then gave nine life sentences to an IRA man who killed nine people by accident. The bomb went off early and even killed one of the men carrying it; the victims were customers in a fish shop next door to the Ulster Defence Force headquarters. The intention of the IRA was to empty the fish shop and destroy the UDF headquarters. It was never their intention to kill anyone in the fish shop at all. They even apologized. For 25 years, the IRA regularly apologized for killing civilians. What's nine people killed by accident in the 20th century? Have the British ever apologized for killing civilians – anywhere, ever?

The Communists probably killed 100 million people, but Communists are respectable. There are Communists everywhere you go. The National Socialists only killed people when they had to, and have been shamed out of existence. Why? Because they offended the Jews on a purely theoretical, philosophical matter: human equality – a myth in which the Jews – the most fanatically racist and race-conscious of all races – have never believed, and have never even intended to practise. Look at Israel.

Hitler called it "National Socialism". Stalin called it "Socialism in One Country". "Socialism" is a dirty word in America, so we'll call it something different. Any stick will do to beat a dog.

1995–2001

ON THE GULF WAR

On January 17, 1991, the United States began an unprovoked war of aggression against Iraq, causing hundreds of thousands of civilian deaths (OK – how many people do YOU say were killed in 100,000 air raids?); hundreds of billions of dollars worth of property damage; incalculable ecological and environmental damage; and a civil war in Iraq, as a result of which millions of people are now refugees.

The pretext for this was an act of "aggression" by Iraq against Kuwait, i.e., that some Arab billionaires had lost a fraction of their personal wealth (most of which is invested abroad). I weep for you, the Walrus said, I deeply sympathize.

In reality, nobody cares about Kuwait; nobody cares about Arabs; and nobody cares which Arab sells us our oil. There is only one thing Americans care about, and that is Jews.

The Gulf War was a war to destroy everything standing in the way of Israeli domination of the Middle East, and Jewish domination of American and European political and cultural life.

This was made possible by two lies: a religious lie, that Jews are God's Chosen People, and a historical lie, that Hitler gassed Six Million Jews.

The first is made possible by Christianity; the second is made possible by Jewish control of the mass media.

Under legislation written by Jews, causing "mental harm" to an ethical, racial, national, or religious group is a "Hate Crime" which causes "suffering" and constitutes an attack upon human dignity.

At some suitable distance, however, the same ethical, racial, national, or religious group, for example, Iraqis, may be killed, maimed, crushed to death under collapsing buildings or blown to bits.

Thus, the criterion is one of mileage: morality varies inversely to the proximity of the "suffering".

The minimum mileage required is presumably that at which screams of pain become inaudible without Jewish Electronic Amplification (JAMP).

Now. I have been looking at a globe, and I find that Israel is really quite far away, in fact, almost as far away as Iraq (it is even further if you travel the other way.)

On this basis, all that is required is a pretext, i.e., an act of "aggression" by Israel, and that nation of self-pitying, hysterical cowards may be disposed of quite inexpensively – since with one bomb, half the country would have a heart attack.

So the question arises, what constitutes "aggression"?

Well, as luck will have it, nothing in international law defines "aggression", and all attempts to define "aggression" have failed.

Nothing in the Briand-Kellogg Pact which "outlawed war" in 1928 defined "aggression"; nothing in the Nuremberg Charter defined "aggression"; nothing in the U.N. Charter defines "aggression".

"I pledge allegiance to the Flag, of the United States of Torture. And to the gulags and secret prisons for which it stands, One nation, under Fear, with Zionist subjugation and slavery for all."

Thus, aggression is anything we want it to be, and everybody else is an "aggressor" if we say so!

This simplifies things.

For example:

If Panama invaded the U.S. and kidnapped President Bush in violation of the USA-Panama extradition treaty, Panama would be the aggressor. The contrary does not make the U.S. an aggressor.

If Iraq bombed Washington to punish us for our aggression against Panama, Iraq would be the aggressor. The contrary does not make the US the aggressor.

To American service personnel, I have only this to say: If you are stupid enough to put on a JOG [Jewish Occupation Government] uniform and leave your family and go thousands of miles away and kill thousands of people just to please the Jews, well, I hope you get killed. If not this time, the next.

I am sorry if that offends some people, but that is my opinion and I will stick with it.

Hitler was right when he said *"The victor in war will not be asked whether he told the truth."* This is an authentic statement, from Defence Document RA-27.

Paradoxically, the slogan of "Operation Desert Storm" – *"Mess with the Best, Die Like the Rest"* – is not considered in violation of the Genocide Convention or national "Hate Laws", provided that the "Best" is not taken to mean or to include the White Race.

To which I say, why shouldn't the White Race be the "Best"?

My dictionary defines "Aryanism" as a belief that the Aryan race possesses superior, if not unique, capacities for government, social organization, and civilization, not to mention science, technology, and medicine. To me, this is a proposition so obvious as to require no proof.

There is another subtlety I am unable to fathom. If I blow up a building with a pipe bomb and kill 2 or 3 people, I am a "terrorist".

If I fly over a city and flatten it with napalm, phosphorous, and cluster bombs, killing 2 or 3 hundred thousand people, I am a "war hero" and worthy of praise.

If this is so, I prefer terrorists: they kill fewer people.

[Recommended reading: *The Fire This Time* by Ramsey Clark.]

1991

PSEUDOZOOLOGICAL SATIRE #1

The lowest form of life exhibiting bilateral symmetry, the Great American Iggernus became extinct early in the 21st century.

Known to naturalists for two pairs of bulbous protrusions or excrescences on the ventral and dorsal surfaces of the body. Those on the ventral surface, in a parallel horizontal arrangement, known as "*lips*", were used to demand welfare and other privileges, while those on the dorsal surface, in a vertical-horizontal arrangement, known as "*buttocks*", supported the weight of the body on Affirmative Action jobs.

Two pairs of matched appendages, known as "*arms and legs*", were used to pursue and grasp joggers and other prey; the organs of reproduction, located along the midline of the ventral surface, were used to commit rape and other crimes.

Habitat: Street corners and everywhere else it was not wanted.

Believed to have been rendered extinct by Mexicans in the belief that automobile seat covers could be manufactured out of "*nigger hide*". They must have been thinking of "*Naugahyde*". Sorry about that.

"*...[T]oo honest or too proud to feign, a love he never cherished...*"

1996

PSEUDOZOOLOGICAL SATIRE #2

Unendangered Species of Today

Noted for its parasitic feeding habits aided by a prehensile proboscis and sharp claws, *Heebus jeebicus* is also remarkable for its extraordinarily thin skin and tall tail, or *Holocauda*.

Cunning and cowardly in nature, *H. jeebicus* is adept at provoking larger animals into combat with each other, while stealing provender from them both.

The subterfuge employed to accomplish such a result is the so-called HOLOCAUST (from the Greek *holos*, total + German *Kot*, excrement, or possibly *kotzen*, to vomit).

The HOLOCAUST tall tale is intended to intimate that whenever people "*hate*" (i.e., whenever racial differences are recognized and discussed), Jews are eventually murdered (allegedly a great loss for Mankind).

According to this theory, Jews, the arbiters of all morality (i.e., they stick their noses into every body else's business), are the eternal victims of all "*hatred*", a belief gratifying their masochism, self-pity, and paranoid schizophrenic tendencies.

I have discussed the HOLOCAUST in a modest booknik, *Made in Russia – The Holocaust*, together with a video of the same name; both are basically a photocopy reproduction of prosecution evidence, testimony, and documents from the First Nuremberg Trial, "proving" a load of lies that nobody believes any more: like steaming and frying people to death in special "steam chamber", and "frying chambers", killing 840,000 Russians in 30 days with a pedal-driven brain-bashing machine (i.e., worked by one foot; it worked like a bicycle, but it had only one pedal), and making socks out of Jew Hair.

The cover of *Made In Russia – The Holocaust* (or *MIRTH* for short) shows two happy, healthy, well-groomed and well-fed individuals, one of them wearing a wrist watch and the other holding a towel, sitting in front of a swimming pool diving board. The high dive is clearly visible behind them. The text reveals that this is a detail taken from a larger photo, which is also reproduced, showing concentration camp inmates, all of them healthy and some of them overweight, at Mauthausen, a notorious concentration camp alleged to have been equipped with "gas chambers", taken after the Liberation, on May 8, 1945.

These are the people who scream that they were mistreated, tortured and gassed, to anyone who will listen.

Contrary to my anticipations, *H. jeebicus* failed to respond with his usual explosion of incoherent fury.

Instead, people called me to say, "*Gee golly, your book is absolutely amazing. Did the Germans really have pedal-driven brain-bashing machines to make human soap? Did they really make socks out of Jew hair?*"

When I told them the book was nothing more than a collection of obvious lies, they couldn't quite understand. People are stupider than I thought. Result: Very poor book sales.

Dismayed by this lack of appreciation (an honour is always without profit in its own country) I wrote to the authorities in Canada, including the public prosecutor's office, expressing the opinion that unprovoked physical attacks and persecution were the best thing that could happen to an ideological movement of any kind. Had they put *MIRTH* on their list of banned "hate materials"? If not, could they remedy this situation as soon as possible? Also, could they arrange for a little raid on my office, with the usual headlines about how I am a bigot, fascist, hater, Nazi, liar, etc. etc. Just a little bit?

The result was a sarcastic letter in which they said they hoped that that I would be successful in provoking someone else into persecuting me. What we have here is a failure to communicate.

Regarding the socks made of Jew hair ("proven" at Nuremberg with Soviet forgeries) I was able to show that Negro hair may be felted (and thus made into socks) but that other hair cannot be felted.

I sometimes amuse myself imagining a couple of "Master Race American Style" soldiers trying on a pair of this *"evidence"*, which no one has ever seen, but which was believed nonetheless:

RUFUS: *Man, whuffo' yo' got them ugly lookin' thangs on yo' feets??!!*

RASTUS: *Hey man, dat be de human hair socks whut be made out ob Jew hair!*

RUFUS: *Man, yo' sho' is stupid. Ain't you hip, dat Nee-gro hair can be felted, but dat uddah hair cain't nebba be felted? Dat on account ob how nigga hair be flat; issue fum de epidermis at a right angle, be spirally twisted, widdout de central duckt. Hair itself be covered wid plenty ob rough, pointed filaments whut adhere loosely to de shaf' ob de hair. Dat be de reason fo' dat deah.*

RASTUS: *Mus' hab been took fum sum ob dem black Jews we's allus hearin' 'bout.*

RUFUS: *Sho' nuff! Y'all got soul socks!*
(Tap dances)
*Fo' a fingah-poppin', foot-hoppin',
Feelin' in yo' feet,
Soviet evidence can't be beat
Slip dat evidence on yo' feet,
Go cool-walkin', jive-talkin'
Down de street. WHUT??!!!*
RASTUS: *Mah athlete's foot got dandruff!!!*

Parenthetically, it appears that the woolly hair of the Negro, associated with special sweat glands, is an adaptation to the heat of a tropical climate (see *1928 Encyclopaedia Britannica*, "Evolution of Man").

While we are on the subject, we all know that scientists can determine the sex of a skeleton (for example, an unidentified murder victim), but can they determine the race of a skeleton?

Well, of course, they can. One of the standard tests is, or used to be, to fill the cranium with sand or shot, then pour the sand or shot into a measured beaker to determine the cranial capacity, since races differ in the size of their brains. Tables of comparative brain sizes may be found in many books on forensic science – such as *Legal Medicine and Toxicology* by Many Specialists; Edited by Frederick A. Frederick A. Peterson D.M., LL.D., Walter S. Haines, A.M., M.D., and Ralph W. Webster, M.D, Ph.D., Philadelphia and London, W.B. Saunders Company, Second Edition, 1923, vol. I, pp. 140-142.

The white man has a very large brain in relation to his body size, and a much more complex brain structure.

The cranial capacity of a microcephalic idiot is about 1000 cubic centimetres, probably the minimum viable brain size for a human being. By contrast, the largest gorilla brain rarely exceeds 600 cc and is usually less; a chimpanzee brain is about 390 cc. *Pithecanthropus erectus* possessed an extremely primitive brain of about 900 cc, while *Rhodesian Man* (a prehistoric jungle bunny only 200,000 years old) had a cranial capacity of about 1200 cc. An Australian aborigine possesses a massive cranium with an extremely small brain case of about 1350 cc, while the Neanderthal and Cro-Magnon cave men in Europe possessed brains of about 1500 cc, equal to that of modern Europeans. Therefore, the most primitive members of the Negro race today possess a cranial capacity somewhere between that of a pin-headed idiot and a European cave man. This has been upgraded somewhat by interbreeding with other races, to the immense loss of the White Race, which receives no benefit for the genetic material lost.

Since realism on the subject of race renders one *ipso facto* criminal, let us move on to a legal subject. Under the Hobbes and Travel Acts, a simple act such as riding on a Greyhound bus (*"interstate travel in furtherance of a criminal enterprise"*) or – if you don't leave the state – making a phone call (*"using an interstate facility in furtherance of a criminal enterprise"*), or worse yet, two phone calls (a *"pattern of racketeering"*, or, perhaps, by way of variation, *"two substantive counts of wire fraud"*, or, even worse, *"engaging in an ongoing activity making use of interstate facilities"*), can lead to very long prison sentences (20-40 years), which may run consecutively with counts for *"conspiracy"*, *"aiding and abetting"*, and *"engaging in a pattern of activity"* (5 years per count).

Remember that the authorities don't need a conviction to charge you with these *"substantive offences"*; all they want is a pretext to obtain an indictment. You can be ACQUITTED of the *"substantive offences"* and still be convicted of *"using an interstate facility"* or *"engaging in a pattern of activity"*, or *"conspiracy"*.

JOG – the Jewish Occupation Government – doesn't need a

conviction for anything on the indictment (they get the indictment just by calling one Grand Jury after another until they get one that will agree to indict you). The trick, from their point of view, is to get as many counts on the indictment as possible, then plea bargain. So, to avoid risking 60 years, or even 80, or 150, you plead guilty to 5 years, and serve 2 – for nothing – for "*using an interstate facility*".

Don't talk to me about "*the land of the free*", it's the Land of the Talmud. Any resemblance to the procedures used at Nuremberg is deliberate and intentional, and all such "crimes" are purely verbal. For example, double jeopardy is prohibited by the Constitution of the United States. So the Jews invent 5 different names for the same thing and turn it into 5 crimes, even if they never existed before. For example, you rob a state bank protected by the Federal Bank Deposit Insurance Corporation; that's two crimes: "state" bank robbery and "Federal" bank robbery. You might get 2 years for state, and 5 years for Federal – consecutively. They'll move you to a Federal prison when you complete the "state" part of your sentence. But you only robbed one bank. Maybe you got one hundred dollars, a thousand if you're lucky.

Generally, you should NEVER PLEAD GUILTY, because it makes appeal infinitely more difficult.

Remember that the Fifth Amendment is personal, and cannot be claimed to avoid incriminating other people. If it is apparent that your answers will incriminate others, you will not be permitted to claim your right to remain silent at that point. You must REFUSE TO ANSWER ANY QUESTIONS PERIOD, AND AGREE TO NOTHING. The Fifth Amendment or privilege against self-incrimination should be claimed explicitly by name.

Remember than an unsworn false statement to a Federal officer is a felony punishable by five year's imprisonment and a $10,000 fine (Title 18, "False Statements"). Of course, they're the only witnesses to what you said, so DON'T TALK TO THEM. Many people carry a typed card saying "I decline to submit to any interrogation on the grounds that it may tend to incriminate me. If I am free to go, I am going. GOODBYE. If I am under arrest, I want a lawyer. My lawyer's name is... I want to see my lawyer RIGHT NOW. I refuse to submit to ANY interrogation so DON'T TALK TO ME". You pull it out and hand it to them. Then you LEAVE IF YOU ARE FREE TO GO, AND IF NOT, SHUT UP.

Finally, remember: Most people who are convicted are convicted ONLY and SOLELY because they TALKED TO SOMEONE ABOUT THE CASE: NO OTHER REASON.

That the Jews are well aware that Hitler was legally elected is reflected in their current efforts to criminalize legitimate political and racial expression as "Race Hatred", a term applied to all actions undertaken by persons of European descent claiming equal protection under the Genocide Convention and the Civil Rights laws.

According to this theory, racial hatred – R.H. for short – is *more horrible than halitosis – more dreadful than B.O. – a greater threat to civilization than dandruff or the atomic bomb*; yet abhorrence, abomination, antipathy, detestation, and loathing are still legal; a point not to be forgotten.

Nor is it a *crimen atrocissimus* to "hate" New York in June, or a Gershwin tune, or Brussels sprouts. However, in compliance with the law, and out of a respect for the sensibilities of those whose melanism approaches the energy wavelength absorbance extreme of the achromatic spectrum – *sho' nuff!* – I shall henceforth eschew vulgar and offensive colloquialisms such as "*nigger*", in favour of the Latin *terminus technicus Iggernus* (of the variety *Iggernus vulgaris*).

May it please the Court.

[Sources of information: *Criminal Defense Techniques*, edited by Sidney Bernstein and Robert M. Cipes, Matthew Bender Books. See also *Race* by John R. Baker.]

1991

REPLY TO AN ENGLISH ANTI-ANTI-SEMITE

Dear Sir or Madame,

Thank you for your letter regarding my alleged *"anti-Semitism"*.

I trust that I am not so lacking in sense or feeling as to be capable of such a sentiment as anti-Semitism.

Fortunately, however, while hatred of Jews is illegal, immoral, and fattening, no law yet forbids us to hate the English.

It appears that the *"crime"* of anti-British *"hatred"* – if it existed – would be committed by a very great many people.

In 1982, the nation that would never dare to "provoke" Negro rioters by squirting water on them – *"racialism"*!!! – sank a ship carrying 1200 naval conscripts in a fight over two rocks the British had forgotten they had.

The ship in question, the *Belgrano* (ex-*USS Phoenix*, built in 1939), was so old that it was to be turned into a museum at the end of the year; was armed with a single gun with a 14-mile range, as against the 20-mile range of guns on British warships; and was sunk without warning, without declaration of war, in international waters – i.e., outside the 200-mile British so-called "exclusion zone" – with two torpedoes from a nuclear submarine, while heading back to Argentina! The officer responsible for the sinking, Capt. Wreford-Browne, returned to Britain as a "war hero", and was rewarded with a medal.

"DID 1200 ARGIES DROWN?"

"GOTCHA!"

[headlines in British tabloid press, i.e., *The Sun*, etc.]

Prior to this incident, in which 366 Argentineans were burned alive or drowned, and which was obviously calculated simply to start a war, not a single British subject had yet been killed, because the Argentineans took the Falklands by firing their weapons in the air after 17 years of negotiations, although they were killed by the dozens in so doing (source of information: *Financial Times*, 3 April 1982. Other sources dispute this, and maintain that only one Argentinean was killed. What is beyond dispute is that no British subjects had yet been killed).

The British then complained that the Argies were using

"*kamikaze*" tactics. It is beyond the comprehension of the British that their actions cause others to hate them.

The IRA then killed 11 British soldiers in two bombings.
(*"WERE 11 BRITS BLOWN TO BITS"? "GOTCHA!"*)

"*Murderous and cowardly*!!!", screamed the Brits, "*a massacre without mercy*!!!" [quotation from Margaret Thatcher, the only Prime Minister in history to cry in the House of Commons when her own son got lost in the desert with his girlfriend during a car race].

Whether that is murder, I leave to you; but cowardly it most certainly it was not. The British will never understand why their enemies always accuse them of hypocrisy.

Inflicting suffering on others is a form of entertainment in Britain; it is called "*aggro*". But it is considered an injustice to be on the receiving end, even 1%.

Mothers of soldiers killed by the IRA are pictured weeping; but others feel the same way too.

The Brits forget that; no matter.

Britain is great again!!! Brits rule OK!!! With a boot in the groin.

Having proven their "greatness" by murdering hundreds of foreigners on the South Pole, the most degenerate nation in Europe may now devote itself to serious matters. These are, in order of importance:

a) kissing the ass of black immigrants and giving them millions of pounds;

b) getting drunk as pigs at football games and killing and injuring people; and

c) telling everybody how "*caring*" they are.

Fortunately, there is a political party operating legally in the United Kingdom – Sinn Fein, 55 Falls Road, Belfast – whose aim is the extirpation, within certain narrow limits, of this noxious breed of humanity.

I trust this meets with your approval, since it is not "*anti-Semitic*."

Yours,
Carlos W. Porter
1982

* * *

Another woman sent me a lengthy "poem" written upon the birth of her infant son.

Synopsis: In the past, she had always hoped that her son would fight for his country, but now she didn't any more, because she was afraid that some people might not be "*grateful*" (!).

I replied in a single sentence, as follows:

"Dear Mrs. Rogers,

I consider it highly unlikely that your son will be conscripted into the naval forces of a South American country only to be murdered by the English, but if that should occur, I can only hope the Argies will be duly grateful."

[Note: The relevance of the above discussion is that it is untrue that we cannot "hate" people; we can "hate" them as much as we like, and we can kill them by the millions. We just cannot protest the Jewish role in the destruction of civilization. (Also, it helps to be a Marxist.)]

STANDARD "HATE" ACCUSATION REPLY FORM

Rap lyrics compiled by "Byron", with comments by C.W. Porter. Stolen from http://tightrope.cc, with many thanks.

* * *

Dear Sir or Madame,
    Thank you very much for your e-mail concerning our "hate", which has received our full attention.
    We feel that perhaps there is some error involved, as you are obviously directing your complaint to the wrong department.
    In view of the following:

[BEGINNING OF THE QUOTES]

    "Kill the white people; we gonna make them hurt; kill the white people; but buy my record first; ha, ha, ha";
    "Kill d'White People"; – Apache, Apache Ain't Shit, 1993, Tommy Boy Music, Time Warner, USA.
    Denver, CO – A white female teenager, Brandy Duval, is raped, sodomized, tortured with a broomstick and stabbed 28 times by a gang of six blacks and Hispanics. Her skull is caved in and corpse dumped into a ditch. Police confiscate a blood soaked mattress as evidence. The murder trial started on the same day as the James Byrd trial!
    "Niggas in the church say: kill whitey all night long. ... the white man is the devil. ... the CRIPS and Bloods are soldiers I'm recruiting with no dispute; drive-by shooting on this white genetic mutant. ... let's go and kill some rednecks. ... Menace Clan ain't afraid. ... I got the .380; the homies think I'm crazy because I shot a white baby; I said; I said; I said: kill whitey all night long. ... a nigga dumping on your white ass; fuck this rap shit, nigga, I'm gonna blast. ... I beat a white boy to the motherfucking ground";
    "Kill Whitey"; – Menace Clan, Da Hood, 1995, Rap-A-Lot Records, Noo Trybe Records, subsidiaries of what was called Thorn EMI and now is called The EMI Group, United Kingdom.
    "Devils fear this brand new shit. ... I bleed them next time I see

them. ... I prey on these devils. ... look what it has come to; who you gonna run to when we get to mobbing. ... filling his body up with lead, yah; cracker in my way; slitting, slit his throat; watch his body shake; watch his body shake; that's how we do it in the motherfucking [San Francisco] Bay. ... Sitting on the dock of the dirty with my AK";

"Heat-featuring Jet and Spice1"; – Paris, Unleashed, 1998, Unleashed Records, Whirling Records.

Killeen, TX – A white couple, Todd and Stacy Bagley are kidnapped on the way to church, set on fire, burned to death and shot in the head by four blacks.

"These devils make me sick; I love to fill them full of holes; kill them all in the daytime, broad motherfucking daylight; 12 o'clock, grab the Glock; why wait for night";

"Sweatin Bullets"; – Brand Nubian, Everything Is Everything, 1994, Elektra Entertainment, Warner Communications, Time Warner, USA.

"A fight, a fight, a nigger and a white, if the nigger don't win then we all jump in. ... smoking all [of] America's white boys";

– "A Fight"; Apache, Apache Ain't Shit, 1993, Tommy Boy Music, Time Warner, USA.

Flint, Michigan – Three white teenagers, Michael Carter, Dustin Kaiser and (girl's name withheld by police) are attacked by six black youths. Carter is shot and killed. Kaiser is beaten and shot in the head, but recovers. The girl is forced to perform oral sex on her black attackers, pistol whipped and shot in the face.

"I kill a devil right now. ... I say kill whitey all nightey long. ... I stabbed a fucking Jew with a steeple. ... I would kill a cracker for nothing, just for the fuck of it. ... Menace Clan kill a cracker; jack 'em even quicker. ... catch that devil slipping; blow his fucking brains out";

"Fuck a Record Deal"; – Menace Clan, Da Hood, 1995, Rap-A-Lot Records, Noo Trybe Records, subsidiaries of Thorn EMI; called The EMI Group since 1997, United Kingdom.

South Carolina – A white female, Melissa McLaughlin, is raped, tortured and skinned alive in a tub of bleach by seven blacks.

"Now I'm black but black people trip 'cause white people like me; white people like me I but don't like them. ... I don't hate whites, I just gotta death wish for motherfuckers that ain't right";

– "Race War"; Ice-T, Home Invasion, 1993, Priority Records, Thorn EMI; now called The EMI Group, United Kingdom.

"To all my Universal Soldier's: stay at attention while I strategize an invasion; the mission be assassination, snipers hitting Caucasians with semi-automatic shots heard around the world; my plot is to control the globe and hold the world hostage. ... see, I got a war plan more deadlier than Hitler. ... lyrical specialist, underworld terrorist. ... keep the unity thick like mud. ... I pulling out gats, launching deadly attacks";

– "Blood for Blood"; Killarmy, Silent Weapons for Quiet Wars, 1997, Wu-Tang Records, Priority Records, The EMI Group, United Kingdom.

Jacksonville, FL – A mentally retarded white man, Gregory Griffith, is beaten and stomped unconscious by blacks and died a few days later. The blacks admitted to the police beating Griffith because "he was white".

"Lead to the head of you devils";

"Lick Dem Muthaphuckas-Remix"; – Brand Nubian, Everything Is Everything, 1994, Elektra Entertainment, Warner Communications, Time Warner, USA.

"This will all be over in '99, so, niggas, give devils the crime; gonna be more devils dying";

– "No Surrender"; Bone Thugs-N-Harmony, Creepin on ah Come Up, 1994, Ruthless Records, Epic Records, Sony Music Entertainment, Sony, Japan.

Kansas City, MO – A black male shoots two white co-workers, Michael Scott and Traci Riehle. Scott is killed and Riehle is critically injured. Police find a note referring to "blood sucker supreme white people".

"Won't be satisfied until the devils-I see them all dead. ... my brother is sending me more guns from down South. ... pale face. ... it's all about brothers rising up, wising up, sizing up our situation. ... you be fucking with my turf when you be fucking with my race; now face your maker and take your last breath; the time is half-past death. ... it's the Armageddon. ... go into the garage; find that old camouflage. ... cracker-shooting nightly";

– "What the Fuck"; Brand Nubian, Everything Is Everything, 1994, Elektra Entertainment, Warner Communications, Time Warner, USA.

".44 ways to get paid. ... I'm through with talking to these devils; now I'm ready to blast";

– "44 Wayz-featuring Mystic"; Paris, Unleashed, 1998, Unleashed Records, Whirling Records.

Alexandria, VA – An eight year old white child, Kevin Shiffiet, is killed when his throat is slit by a black who also stabs his 80 year old great grandmother and punches her in the chest. Police find a hand rambling note stating. "Kill them raceess whiate kidd's anyway".

"Like my niggas from South Central Los Angeles they found that they couldn't handle us; Bloods, CRIPS, on the same squad, with the Essays up, and nigga, it's time to rob and mob and break the white man off something lovely";

– "The Day the Niggaz Took Over"; Dr Dre, The Chronic, 1993, Interscope Records, under Time Warner in 1993.

Burlington, NC – A ten year old white child, Tiffany Long, is raped, sodomized, sexually tortured and murdered by two black males and a black female. The black female rams a broomstick up her vagina and rectum. The parents were prohibited from seeing their dead daughter's body.

"Bust a Glock; devils get shot. ... when God give the word me herd like the buffalo through the neighborhood; watch me blast. ... I'm killing more crackers than Bosnia-Herzegovina, each and everyday. ... don't bust until you see the whites of his eyes, the whites of his skin. ... Louis Farrakhan ... Bloods and CRIPS, and little old me, and we all getting ready for the enemy";

– "Enemy"; Ice Cube, Lethal Injection, 1993, Priority Records, Thorn EMI; now called The EMI Group, United Kingdom.

"Devil, to gangbanging there's a positive side and the positive side is this-sooner than later the brothers will come to Islam, and they will be the soldiers for the war; what war, you ask; Armageddon; ha, ha, ha, ha, ha";

"Armageddon"; – RBX, The RBX Files, 1995, Premeditated Records, Warner Brother Records, Time Warner, USA.

"Subtract the devils that get smoked. ... we're people, black people; steal your mind back, don't die in their wilderness. ... let's point our heaters the other way";

– "Dial 7"; Digable Planets, Blowout Comb, 1994, Pendulum Records, Thorn EMI; now called The EMI Group, United Kingdom.

"Get them devil-made guns and leave them demons bleeding; give them back whips, and just feed them bullets";

– "Wicked Ways"; Sunz of Man, One Million Strong: The Album, 1995, Mergela Records, Solar/Hines Co., Prolific Records.

Fayetteville, NC – Two white women, Tracy Lambert and Susan Moore, are carjacked by a group of seven blacks and Hispanics and shot execution style in the head. This murder was part of a gang initiation. The bullets found in the victims' heads were painted blue, the Crips' gang color.

"It's time to send the devil to the essence... this is a must because there ain't no reform or trust; you got a Glock and you see a devil, bust... . they'll be calling us the trigger men, the nappy-knotty red-beard devil-assassin; Lord make a law; at midnight I'll be bashing. ... field niggas [are] locked in until 2005";

– "Field Nigguhz in a Huddle"; Professor Griff, Blood of the Prophet; 1998, Lethal Records, Mercury Records, PolyGram, Phillips' Electronics NV, Netherlands. PolyGram merged with Universal Music

Group in 1998, the parent being The Seagram Company of Canada, owned by Edgar Bronfman.

Alton, Illinois – A white male, Richard Skelton, is attacked and stomped to death by a group of 25 blacks while black onlookers yell, "Kill the cracker".

"He preys on old white ladies [who] drive the Mercedes with the windows cracked. ... you should've heard the bitch screaming. ... sticking guns in crackers' mouths. ... the cops can't stop it. ... remember 4-29-92, come on; Florence and Normandy coming to a corner near you, cracker; we've been through your area, mass hysteria; led by your motherfucking Menace Clan";

– "Mad Nigga"; Menace Clan, Da Hood, 1995, Rap-A-Lot Records, Noo Trybe Records, Time Warner, USA.

"The black man is god. ... buy a Tec [and] let loose in the Vatican... I love the black faces; so put your Bible in the attic";

– "Ain't No Mystery"; Brand Nubian, In God We Trust, 1992, Elektra Entertainment, Warner Communications, Time Warner, USA.

Cleveland, OH – A five year old white girl, Devon Duniver, was stabbed to death by a black teenager who said after the murder, "She got what she deserved."

"Rhymes is rugged like burnt buildings in Harlem; the Ol Dirty Bastard. ... I'm also militant. ... snatching devils up by the hair, then cut his head off";

– "Cuttin Headz"; Ol Dirty Bastard, Return of the 36 Chambers: the Dirty Version; 1995, Elektra Entertainment, Time Warner, USA.

Kansas City, MO – A six year old white child, Jake Robel, is dragged to death by a black carjacker who drove away even as the boy being dragged screamed outside of the car door while still partially attached to the seat belt.

"Listen to this black visionary, bringing war like a revolutionary. ... go on a killing spree, putting devils out their misery; hearing screams, sounds of agony; my hostility takes over me. ... camouflaged ninjas avenging";

– "Under Siege"; Killarmy, Silent Weapons for Quiet Wars, 1997, Wu-Tang Records, Priority Records, The EMI Group, United Kingdom.

"Swing by on the pale guy. ... break him in the neck. ... the guerrilla with the poison tip. ... shaking pinky up on a dull-ass ice-pick... this is Lench Mob. ... devil, what you want to do; when you see the boot, knew your head is hoohoo ";

– "King of the Jungle"; Da Lench Mob, Planet of da Apes,

1994, Priority Records, Thorn EMI; now called The EMI Group, United Kingdom.

Buffalo, NY – A white man, Gary Traska, is stomped to death by three blacks. Many of his organs were actually split apart from the savage beating.

"Dropping verses, casting curses, throwing these hexes on the devils. ... respect to Farrakhan, but I'm the jungle-don, the new guerrilla, top-ranked honky killer. ... what do blacks do; they just keep on blowing devils away. ... evil fucking cracker. ... I'm tightening up the laces to my steel-toed boots, so I can walk, stomp; we stomp this devil down in the park";

– "Planet of da Apes"; Da Lench Mob, Planet of da Apes, 1994, Priority Records, Thorn EMI; now called The EMI Group, United Kingdom.

Fayetteville, NC – A white male, Donald Lange, is stomped by ten black males. Lange is now brain dead and a complete vegetable.

"We're having thoughts of overthrowing the government. ... the brothers and sisters threw their fists in the air. ... it's open season on crackers, you know; the morgue will be full of Caucasian John Doe's. ... I make the Riot shit look like a fairy tale. ... oh my god, Allah, have mercy; I'm killing them devils because they're not worthy to walk the earth with the original black man; they must be forgetting; it's time for Armageddon, and I won't rest until they're all dead";

– "Goin Bananas"; Da Lench Mob, Planet of da Apes, 1994, Priority Records, Thorn EMI; now called The EMI Group, United Kingdom.

Salt Lake City, UT – A black man breaks into the house of two white women, Amy Clinton and Aaron Warren. The black man stabs both women, killing Amy Clinton and seriously injuring Aaron Warren.

"The crackers ain't shit; chase them out of the jungle; now raise up off the planet. ... we get the 12 gauge; shot to the chest. ... we hitting devils up. ... Da Lench Mob, environmental terrorist. ... I gripped the Glock and had to knock his head from his shoulders. ... I got the .30[6] on the rooftop; pop; pop; so many devils die. ... make sure I kill them... lynch a thousand a week if it's necessary";

– "Environmental Terrorist"; Da Lench Mob, Planet of da Apes, 1994, Priority Records, Thorn EMI; now called The EMI Group, United Kingdom.

Bloomington, IL – A white female, Patricia Stansfield is dragged two miles to her death during a carjacking by a black male.

"Like an armed struggle. ... I come with the New Wu Order. ... waging war on the devils' community. ... whipped cardinals and one

Pope";

– "Universal Soldiers"; Killarmy, Silent Weapons for Quiet Wars, 1997, Wu-Tang Records, Priority Records, The EMI Group, United Kingdom.

"Swinging out of the trees, is the blood-spilling, devil-killing, nappy-headed g.'s . ... blacks and Mexicans must take a stand. ... I'm down with Chico, and not with the man";

– "Set the Shit Straight"; Da Lench Mob, Planet of da Apes, 1994, Priority Records, Thorn EMI; now called The EMI Group, United Kingdom.

Reno, NV – A Polynesian immigrant kills a white police officer, George Sullivan, with a hatchet. Sullivan is struck 20 times. The immigrant admits to killing Sullivan because "he was a white police officer".

"Fuck them laws, because the Mob is coming raw; nigga, is you down because it's the Final Call. ... grab your gat; know the three will start busting; I'm trying to take them down. ... the war of wars with no fucking scores. ... April 29 was a chance to realize ... the g.'s are out to kill. ... we got crackers to kill; sending them back in on a ship to Europe. ... they deserve it. ... a nation-wide riot across America. ... this is the Final Call on black man and black woman, rich and poor; rise up";

– "Final Call"; Da Lench Mob, Planet of da Apes, 1994, Priority Records, Thorn EMI; now called The EMI Group, United Kingdom.

"I come with the wicked style. ... I got everybody jumping to the voodoo. ... I got a gat and I'm looking out the window like Malcolm. ... April 29 was power to the people, and we just might see a sequel";

– "Wicked"; Ice Cube, The Predator, 1992, Priority Records, Thorn EMI; now called The EMI Group, United Kingdom.

Boulder, CO – A white college student, "Jane Doe", is gang-raped at gun-point by six Asians. Because of court proceedings and fear of retaliation by the "Asian Crips", she is referred to as "Jane Doe". The Asians admit to raping the girl "because she was blonde and white".

"Deal with the devil with my motherfucking steel. ... white man is something I tried to study, but I got my hands bloody, yeah. ... I met Farrakhan and had dinner";

– "When Will They Shoot"; Ice Cube, The Predator, 1992, Priority Records, Thorn EMI; now called The EMI Group, United Kingdom.

"Actual fact you need to be black. ... everyday I fight a devil. ... I grab a shovel to bury a devil. ... the battle with the beast, Mr. 666. ... my mind rolled to a 7th level; grab my bazooka and nuke a devil. ... with black, I build; for black, I kill";

– "Fightin the Devil"; RBX, The RBX Files, 1995, Premeditated Records, Warner Brother Records, Time Warner, USA.

Racine, WI – A black gang member, Nazeer Ghani, fires into a crowd of white concert-goers while shouting racial epithets, killing father of two Joe Rowan. Although identified by 30 witnesses, police release the killer for "lack of evidence."

"I pledge allegiance to only the black. ... black, you had best prepare for the coming of war. ... look at you devil; now you're sweating; I'm telling you: you can't run from the hand of Armageddon. ... he eats his pig-steak rare so he can taste the blood";

– "No Time"; RBX, The RBX Files, 1995, Premeditated Records, Warner Brother Records, Time Warner, USA.

"Killing devils [and] scatter they ashes over the sea of Mediterranean . ... open your eyes to the revolution. ... unite with the black coalition";

– "Wake Up"; Killarmy, Silent Weapons for Quiet Wars, 1997, Wu-Tang Records, Priority Records, The EMI Group, United Kingdom.

"My own kind blind, brain-trained on the devil-level. ... chasing down loot, Dole or Newt, who do you shoot. ... rough stuff to the babies, spread like rabies";

– "Niggativity ... Do I Dare Disturb the Universe"; Chuck D, Autobiography of MistaChuck, 1996, Mercury Records, PolyGram, Phillips' Electronics NV, Netherlands. PolyGram merged within Universal Music Group in 1998, the parent being The Seagram Company, Canada.

"Buck the devil; boom. ... shoot you with my .22; I got plenty of crew; I take out white boys. ... we got big toys with the one-mile scope, taking whitey's throat";

– "Buck tha Devil"; Da Lench Mob, Guerrillas in tha Mist, 1992, Eastwest Records America, Elektra, Atlantic, Time Warner, USA.

Pine Ridge Indian Reservation, SD – A white man is dragged to his death by Indians. Federal officials hesitate to call it a "hate crime".

"Little devils don't go to heaven. ... the AK forty ... hold a fifty clip, and I'll shoot until it's empty. ... I'm killing only seven million civilians. ... one dead devil";

"Freedom Got an AK"; Da Lench Mob, Guerrillas in tha Mist,

1992, Eastwest Records America, Elektra, Atlantic, Time Warner, USA.

"Grab your deep-ass crews. ... we gotta make them ends, even if it means Jack and friends. ... now you're doomed, hollow-points to the dome; once again it's on. ... out comes my .22. ... I'm the cut-throat; now I got to cut you ... '94 is the season for lynching; from out of the dark is the South Central g., ready-hand steady on a bloody machete. ... a devil is on my shoulder; should I kill it; hell yah. ... I slice Jack. ... took an axe, and gave that bitch, Jill, forty wacks. ... with my hip hop ... it don't stop, until heads roll off the cutting block";

– "Cut Throats"; Da Lench Mob, Planet of da Apes, 1994, Priority Records, Thorn EMI; now called The EMI

Miami, FL – Seven whites are murdered by the Yahweh Cult whose leader orders the members to cut off and return the ears of the victims as proof of the murders. The trial was conducted at the same time as the Rodney King trial!

[END OF THE QUOTES]

– don't you have anything better to do?

Should you wish to pursue the matter, however, we require the following by return e-mail:

a) an objective definition of "hate";

b) an objective showing of why the Ad Hominem Fallacy (with a Freudian twist) should be any more valid today than it was in the days of Aristotle;

c) an objective showing of why my opinions constitute "hate", but the above does not;

d) an objective showing of why my opinions constitute "hate" but YOURS do not.

The Seven Mortal Sins (or Capital Vices) of the traditional Catholic Church are anger, envy, gluttony, greed, lust, pride, sloth.

"Hate" is not mentioned.

The catechism lists the following possible "Mortal Sins": fornication, impurity, licentiousness, idolatry, sorcery, enmity, strife, jealousy, anger, selfishness, dissension, factions, envy, drunkenness, and carousing.

"Hate" is not mentioned.

First Corinthians 6:9-10 (somewhat paraphrased) lists the following as sins denying entry to the Kingdom of Heaven: fornication, idolatry, adultery, male prostitution, thievery, greed, habitual drunkenness, revelry and robbery.

"Hate" is not mentioned.

Luke 12:10 (again, slightly paraphrased) lists blasphemy against the Holy Spirit as the one unforgivable sin.

"Hate" is not mentioned.

Romans 1:29-32 (again, slightly paraphrased) lists the following as deserving death:

Unrighteousness, fornication, wickedness, covetousness, maliciousness, enviousness, murder [note that the same people who favour "hate" laws are also against capital punishment, except perhaps for "anti-Semitism", as in the Soviet Union under Stalin], disputatiousness, deceit, malignity, whispering, backbiting, hatred of God [not "Race Hatred", be it noted], despitefulness, pride, boasting, inventing evil things, disobedience to one's parents, being without understanding, covenant-breaking, being without natural affections, implacability, and mercilessness [the last two being largely specialities of the Jews and the blacks whom the Jews pretend to love so much], and, finally, "Who knowing the judgement of God, that they which commit such things are worthy of death, not only do the same, but have pleasure in them that do them".

With the exception of "hatred of God", "Hate" is not mentioned.

Revelations 21:7-8 lists the following, and I quote:

"The cowardly, the faithless, the polluted, the murderers, the fornicators, the sorcerers, the idolaters, and all liars, their place will be in the lake that burns with fire and sulphur, which is the second death."

"Haters" – or, if you prefer, "race haters" – are not listed.

Revelations 22:15 (somewhat paraphrased) lists the following: sorcery, fornication, murder and idolatry and loving and practising falsehood.

"Hate" is not listed.

Section 1853 of the Catholic catechism states:

"The root of sin is in the heart of man, in his free will, according to the teaching of the Lord: 'For out of the heart come evil thoughts, murder, adultery, fornication, theft, false witness, slander. These are what defile a man.' But in the heart also resides charity, the source of the good and pure works, which sin wounds."

"Hate" is not listed.

The same source quotes Jesus as saying:

"Do not kill, Do not commit adultery, Do not steal, Do not bear false witness, Do not defraud, Honor your father and mother."

"Hate" is not mentioned.

The Catholic catechism, again, lists the following as possible

Mortal Sins, and the following persons as guilty of possible Mortal Sins (the list is somewhat garbled; presumably somebody has been hitting the Communion "vino"):

Abortion,
Anger,
Adultery,
Amending the words of the Holy Bible,
Blasphemy against the Holy Spirit (Eternal sin)
Carousing,
Cowardice,
Defrauders,
Dissensions,
Disrespect towards parents,
Drunkenness,
Enmities,
Envy,
Factions,
Faithless,
False witness (liars)
Fornicators,
Greed,
Holy Communion received while in a state of mortal sin,
Idolatry,
Impurity,
Jealousy,
Licentiousness,
Love and practice falsehoods,
Male prostitution,
Murderers,
Polluted,
Quarrelling,
Sodomites,
Sorcery,
Strife,
Thieves (steal/robbers).

At this rate, of course, we are all culpable, but "Hate" is not listed.

It should be noted that "Enmity" is not synonymous with "Hate".

Robert E. Lee, for example, is said to have been "*a foe without hate, a friend without treachery, a soldier without cruelty, a victim without murmuring... and a man without guile".*

The Jews – the inventors of psychoanalysis – are the world's past masters at evading any and all logical or factual argument and/or analysis. Their response to any situation is to invent some opprobrious but undefined neologism which is then used indiscriminately.

Since the Jews have created the situation described above with their "Civil Rights Laws", "Immigration Laws", their control of the music and entertainment industries and legal professions, and in view of their own treatment of the Palestinians, it is my belief that they are no longer entitled (if indeed they ever were) to use the words "Hate", "Evil", and all the rest of their limitless vocabulary of vituperation, with reference to anyone but themselves.

Faithfully,
Carlos W. Porter

Crazed by "Hoaxoco$t denial denial" (i.e., claims of a "Hoaxoco$t"), this normally mild-mannered individual has become a fanatical "hater" of nationalism, patriotism, Western Civilization and Christianity.

See also "Exterminate Whitey" (security camera footage of blacks beating and killing whites while Martin Luther King raves about "freedom" and "brotherhood" and his "dream" and "de mountaintop").

Yeah, well, I've got a "dream", too – no niggers.

2003–2006

THE ARISTOTELIAN CONNECTION

Written to dispute the contention, popularised in England by Margaret Thatcher and in America by Ayn Rand, that "only individuals exist". "People" exist; the "community" and "nation" do not. Of course, it is all very different when we are "punishing Syria", etc., although we know that only "people" will die; at this point, the "nation" exists, but the "people" do not! Later, when we've killed half of them, the "people" will exist again, so that we can brag about how we've "liberated" half of them from a "brutal dictator"!
    I wonder how this would look in terms of classical philosophy? I think it would go something like this.

* * *

I'm not usually interested in philosophy and I think philosophers are crazy – ("*Can Being Be Posited* [?] *of Non-Being?*" for 20,000 pages, etc. etc.) – but some philosophical problems are important. Take the problem of the nature of abstractions (the idea of "horse" as distinguished from individual horses). This is also known as "the problem of Universals and Particulars".

    Plato taught that abstractions are real, and pre-exist concrete, individual objects, which are simply the "pale reflection" of pre-existing, perfect abstractions. Abstractions are not only perfect, they are more real, and more valuable, than the concrete objects in which they are reflected.

    A scientist might well see the "pre-existing abstraction" in terms of genetic possibility. A Darwinist or National Socialist would say that a horse is evolving towards, or away from, its potential as a "perfect horse", which exists as a biological possibility only. But the view of Platonist idealism goes much further, since it extends to ALL abstractions, i.e., courage, loyalty, honour, books, art, etc.

    Not surprisingly, this view of abstractions is called Idealism (or Nominalism).

    Aristotle, by contrast, taught that abstractions are a product of the human mind: we observe individual horses with their similarities and differences, and arrive at an abstract concept, an imaginary notion of "horse" which exists only in the mind.

    This is called Rationalism. This view of abstractions has been increasingly dominant since the 13th century, and has now triumphed almost absolutely. (Rationalists are very fond of accusing their opponents of "irrationalism", but it should be not noted that Idealists are no more "irrational" than Rationalists at all, partly because the words are used in a special sense, but mainly because the "rationalism" of the Rationalists is essentially a style of argument, a choice of vocabulary.)

Aristotelians are great hair-splitters. For example, they distinguish between "essence" and "accidents". The "essence" of a thing is that which makes it what it is, its "*quiditas*", or "thatness". This does not include its existence. Existence is a non-essential quality, or "accident". A horse can be a horse without existing.

Modern philosophers, in turn, tend to say, "Well, if abstractions exist only in the mind, and if a horse can be a horse without existing, and since we can imagine horses any way we want to: 66 teeth, 19 legs, 4 stomachs, what's left of the concept of 'horse'? Nothing. All you have to do is fiddle around with the definition of words."

Now, on the face of it, it must be admitted that the Platonic view appears nothing less than insane, while the Aristotelian view appears to represent simple common sense. If I say, "There is no such thing as humanity, only individual human beings", or "There is no such thing as mankind, only individual men and women", I appear to be making a self-evident statement of fact. But it is not a fact. It is the expression of a theory of abstractions which dates back to Aristotle.

In fact, the Platonic view is closer to the truth, as I intend to show.

Not only is the Aristotelian view incorrect, it is profoundly destructive and dangerous. One need only repeat the Aristotelian view often enough, taken to sufficiently great extremes, to destroy the basis of all human knowledge.

The fallacy of the Aristotelian view of abstractions becomes obvious if I say, "There is no such thing as courage, only individual acts of courage", or "There is no such thing as the complete works of Shakespeare, only the individual words which make up these works: *wherefore, art, thou*, etc."

Many modern philosophers actually imply as much (for example, the behaviourists or logical positivists), and appear to believe that "anybody can be Shakespeare", as long as we have a computer to shuffle the word combinations around.

Common variants include the following:

– "There is no such thing as the nation, only individual members of the nation".

– "There is no such thing as society, only individual members of society."

– "There is no such thing as the American people, only individual American citizens."

– "There is no such thing as the White Race, only individual white people."

– "There is no such thing as the Negro Race, only individual Negroes."

This is, in fact, the basis for the common assertion that "race" is an unscientific concept. People admit the scientific nature of genetics and heredity on an individual basis, but deny its application to the group, because they deny the existence of the group itself. All modern Aristotelian philosophies are individualistic (anti-nationalist, anti-racialist, anti-traditionalist, anti-patriotic), because they deny the reality of the collective, the nation, the race. If there is "no such thing as the nation", then the nation can have no claims on the individual. (It should be noted that this doesn't prevent individuals from making claims on the nation.)

Indeed, according to this theory, the nation never even existed, except as a geographical entity (varying in size according to the particular historical period) inhabited by individual human beings, from the King on down. To state that an individual should sacrifice himself for the nation is simply to state that some individuals must sacrifice themselves for the sake of other individuals, all of whom are alive at the present time (since dead and future generations exist only as abstract concepts, as a potential).

Hegel said that everything contains within itself the seeds of its opposite. Democracy, for example, begins as "majority rule", as "rule with the consent of the governed", and ends up, inevitably, in the absolute, totalitarian tyranny of minuscule minorities, or even isolated individuals. Dictatorship is the rule of a minority of one. The result: "Democracy", the most oppressive and hysterical political and intellectual straitjacket on the planet, a.k.a. Political Correctness. Two hundred million people, and a single dissenting voice is intolerable.

Note the manner in which the Jews switch back and forth between philosophical systems to suit themselves. In one breath we are told that "There is no such thing as International Jewry" to take responsibility for Jewish crimes (Dresden, the Morgenthau Plan, Zionist atrocities in Palestine, etc; the list is *literally* endless), but there IS such a thing as "the German people" (to be bled white for the so-called "Holocaust"). In the very next breath, we are told that "There is NO such thing as the German people", because "Anybody can be a

German", even a Turk or Congolese!

Another example: "There is no such thing as the Negro Race", to be feared, blamed, and/or hated for their resentfulness, destructiveness, and high crime rates, but there IS such a thing as the "White Race" to feel guilty for slavery! In the very next breath, we told that "There is NO such thing as the White Race", because "Racial purity is a delusion"!

To destroy the anti-pornography laws, the Jews became Aristotelians and split hairs to show that "obscenity", "lasciviousness", and "prurient interest" were meaningless concepts incapable of definition. Then, to destroy Revisionism, they became Platonists, and referred to a pre-existing ideal of perfect social harmony allegedly being damaged by "Hatred", without any definition of terms whatsoever.

The point of the above discussion is to show that National Socialism (which is not limited to the writings or speeches of Adolf Hitler and his followers, but which, on the contrary, has far-ranging philosophical roots) is a serious school of philosophical thought. The National Socialists make a clean sweep of 2000 years of philosophical thought by stating that a human being is subject to the laws of nature. Hitler's statement that *"the ultimate wisdom is the understanding of the instinct"* is in fact one of the profoundest truths ever uttered by any human being. His practical failure does not diminish that fact. No one is diminished by martyrdom.

This makes Hitler one of the greatest philosophical thinkers of all time. Since he was also the greatest social reformer in history, as well as one of history's greatest military and political leaders, this makes him one of the greatest geniuses that ever lived.

Personally, I have been very critical of Hitler in some respects in the past. But as more information becomes available from authentic documents (which exist by the ton, but most of which no one has yet taken the trouble to study), and as our views evolve in reaction to events, I believe that such is the final truth which will ultimately emerge.

It should be noted that "Race" and "Nation" were almost synonymous until fairly recently. To a patriot, it is obvious that the "nation" possesses a reality which extends over thousands of years, both past and present. Not only does the "Nation", as an ideal, possess perfection, it is, in fact, in reality, more real, and more important, than the individuals of which it is said to consist at any given moment.

Let us reject the Aristotelian view of abstractions. Let us state that, for us, as for Plato, abstractions are real.

Let us state that the individual member of the nation is simply the "pale shadow" of the "perfect abstraction" of its greatest men.

Even primitive tribes have their great warriors, priests, scribes, magicians, poets, seers. It is these which make the individual tribesman that which he is. To pretend otherwise is simply unrealistic.

Let us state that we are what the race, the nation, our ancestors, the family, our great political and religious leaders, have made us, and that, without them, we are nothing.

Let us state that it is to them, our ancestors, our countrymen, that we owe everything.

Let us state that, to us, the race, the nation, family, honour, and loyalty are a reality.

Let us state that to this ideal we are duty bound to sacrifice, not only our own lives, but the lives of others as well, if needs be.

It is obvious that abstractions are real. How far would you get in farming if you said, "There is no such thing as varieties of corn, only individual ears of corn"; or "There is no such thing as breeds of cows, only individual Holsteins, Guernseys, etc."?

It is obvious that the "variety" or "breed" is more perfect and more real than the individual ear or animal. The "variety" or "breed" can be improved, and survives eternally, while the individual "ear" or "cow" has only one lifetime, and is gone in a meal. The same is true, *mutatis mutandis*, of the human individual. In Biblical terms, *"he cometh forth as the grass and is cut down"*.

During the Spanish Civil War, on 23 July 1936, the Communists captured the 12-year-old son of the Commanding Officer of the Nationalist garrison in the Alcázar at Toledo, and threatened to shoot him unless the officer surrendered the garrison within 15 minutes. This was over the telephone; the lines hadn't been cut yet. The Nationalist Commander, Gen. José Moscardó, said, "May I speak to him?" The boy was put on the line. Moscardó said, "Hello, what's going on?" The boy said, "Hi, Papá. They say they are going to shoot me if you don't surrender the fortress in 15 minutes". Moscardó said, *"You know how I think. Your father is not going to surrender. If it's true that they're going to shoot you, I want you to commend your soul to Jesus Christ and say your prayers, and I want you to die like a Spaniard... "*. The boy said *"Yes, Papá"*. Moscardó said, *"A kiss for all eternity"*. The boy said, *"Goodbye, Papá"*. Moscardó said, *"Put the officer back on the line"*. The Communist officer came back on the line, and Moscardó said, *"You can save the 15 minutes you offered me, because the Alcázar will never surrender!"* And it didn't.

[The story of the phone conversation is almost undoubtedly a legend, since I do not see how the phone lines could remain uncut 5 days into the rebellion, but it illustrates a moral principle. What is certain is that the boy was held captive outside the fortress, that he died during the siege, and that the fortress never surrendered.]

That was the action of an idealist. His oath, his loyalty, his nation, the lives and freedom of the men under his command, came first. This is where the cerebral spirit of Jewish Aristotelianism gets out its mental slide rule or pocket calculator and draws up a profit and loss account in which "Spain" counts for zero, because the "nation" doesn't exist!

It should be noted that a decision to betray the garrison would have been particularly easy to rationalize. The revolt appeared hopeless and the enemy represented the so-called "legal government" of Spain – a government of Marxists and traitors to whom men of decency no longer owed any loyalty.

1995–2001

* * *

The real Aristotle said, "*A state is not a mere aggregate of persons*" (*Politics*, Book 7, part 7). To the Objectivists and libertarians, it is – and it doesn't even matter who they are.

The latest "Free Market" brainstorm is to bill soldiers for medical care received after being disabled in combat; innocent people for their board bill after spending 25 years in prison for murders they didn't commit, etc. etc.

(Note that if you're *guilty*, you can go to jail for free, but if you're *innocent*, you've got to pay. What could be more Jewish than that?)

As Karl Marx, a Jew himself, said, "*Money is their God.*"

WE LOCKED YOU UP IN JAIL FOR 25 YEARS AND YOU WERE INNOCENT ALL ALONG? THAT'LL BE £80,000 PLEASE

Blunkett charges miscarriage of justice victims 'food and lodgings'
By Neil Mackay, Home Affairs Editor [Sunday Herald, Scotland]

[HEADLINE]:
WHAT DO YOU GIVE SOMEONE WHO'S BEEN PROVEN INNOCENT AFTER SPENDING THE BEST PART OF THEIR

LIFE BEHIND BARS, WRONGFULLY CONVICTED OF A CRIME THEY DIDN'T COMMIT?

An apology, maybe? Counselling? Champagne? Compensation? Well, if you're David Blunkett, the Labour Home Secretary, the choice is simple: you give them a big, fat bill for the cost of board and lodgings for the time they spent freeloading at Her Majesty's Pleasure in British prisons.

On Tuesday, Blunkett will fight in the Royal Courts of Justice in London for the right to charge victims of miscarriages of justice more than £3000 for every year they spent in jail while wrongly convicted. The logic is that the innocent man shouldn't have been in prison eating free porridge and sleeping for nothing under regulation grey blankets.

Blunkett's fight has been described as "outrageous", "morally repugnant" and the "sickest of sick jokes", but his spokesmen in the Home Office say it's a completely "reasonable course of action" as the innocent men and women would have spent the money anyway on food and lodgings if they weren't in prison. The government deems the claw-back *'Saved Living Expenses'*.

Paddy Hill was one of the Birmingham Six. He spent 16 years behind bars for the 1974 Birmingham pub bombings by the IRA. Hill now lives on a farm with his wife and children near Beith in Scotland. He has been charged £50,000 for living expenses by the Home Office.

It wasn't until two years ago that Hill was finally awarded £960,000 in compensation. However, during the years since his release, while waiting for the pay-out, the government had given him advances of around £300,000. When his compensation came through, the £300,000 was taken back along with interest on the interim payments charged at 23% – that cost him a further £70,000.

[Note: They *"advance"* you 300,000 pounds on money they owe you anyway, then when your "final payment" comes through, you are supposed to *repay* the *"advance"* at *23% interest!* At the same time, if you put the money in the bank, you'd probably get 2%! *If this doesn't prove the whole system is Jewish, what does? I wonder what follower of Ayn Rand thought this one up?*]

"The whole system is absurd," Hill said. "I'm so angry about what has happened to me. *I try and tell people about being charged for bed and board in jail and they can't believe it.*

"When I left prison I was given no training for freedom – no counselling or psychological preparation. Yet the guilty get that when they are released. To charge me for the food I ate and the cell I slept in is almost as big an injustice as fitting me up in the first place.

"While I was in prison, my family lost their home, yet they get no compensation. But the state wants its money back. It's like being kicked in the head when someone has beat you already.

"I have to put up with this, yet there has not been one police officer convicted of fitting people up. The Home Office had no shortage of money to keep me in jail or to run a charade of a trial.

"But they had enough money to frame me. Nevertheless, when it comes to paying out compensation for ruining my life they happily rip me to shreds."

Hill is not leading the legal action against the government – instead he has handed the baton to another high-profile victim of miscarriage of justice: Mike O'Brien.

O'Brien spent 10 years in jail wrongly convicted of killing a Cardiff newsagent. His baby daughter died while he was in prison and he was *charged £37,500 by the Home Office for his time behind bars.*

Hill said he cannot lead the legal fight as the Birmingham Six have fought every legal action together, but now three of them are over 70 and Hill believes it is too much to ask them to join him in taking on the government yet again.

He said he was also worried about the compensation payments for the other members of the Birmingham Six being affected if they joined him in court against the government.

"The establishment hate me and people like me as we proved them wrong," he said. "They either want to ignore us or hurt us."

O'Brien took the Home Office to court last March and won, but Blunkett appealed the decision. On Tuesday, the rights and wrongs of the government policy will be decided at the Royal Courts.

O'Brien said: "Morally, the position of the government is just outrageous. It shows total contempt for the victims of miscarriages of justice. It makes me livid.

"I really believe if we win the appeal this week, the government is evil enough to take me to the House of Lords. They are trying to break us. I really think this is personal as far as the government is concerned.

"A government really can't get much worse than this. But I am confident that we will win as the law and morality are on our side."

Vincent Hickey, one of the Bridgewater Four who was wrongly convicted for killing a paperboy, was charged £60,000 for the *17 years* he spent in jail. He said: *"If I had known this I would have stayed on hunger-strike longer, that way I would have had a smaller bill."*

John McManus, of the Scottish Miscarriage of Justice Organisation, said: "This is reprehensible. How can we call ourselves a democratic, civilised society when our government is acting like this?

"The government seems intent on punishing innocent people. *The state wants to be paid for making a mistake.* It's hard to believe someone actually thought this policy up. If you tell a child about this they will think it insane.

"Only a sick mind could have invented this policy, yet the government is fighting to retain the right to act like this. It is cruelty with intent. They seem to want to punish people for having the audacity to be innocent."

The SNP's shadow justice minister, Nicola Sturgeon, said: "This is outrageous. It is another assault by Blunkett on the rule of law and on civil liberties. These people didn't chose to go to prison. They were wrongly convicted, and to charge them for it beggars belief."

The Home Office said an "independent assessor appointed by the Home Secretary takes into account the range of costs the prisoner might have incurred had they not been imprisoned". The spokesman said the assessor was "right" to do this, adding: "Morally, this is reasonable and appropriate."

'I was a hostage, now they are billing me'

ROBERT Brown was just a 19-year-old from Glasgow when he was jailed for life for murdering a woman called Annie Walsh in Manchester in 1977. He served 25 years before he was finally freed in 2002, when the courts ruled him innocent of the crime.

He is now facing a bill of around £80,000 for the living expenses he cost the state. For Brown, it is the final straw. An interim payment he was given pending his full compensation offer is exhausted; his mother recently died; his relationship with his girlfriend has fallen apart and he is facing eviction from his home following a mix-up over benefits.

"I feel like ending my life," he says. "I've tried to maintain my dignity, but the state has treated me with nothing but contempt – *now they are asking me for money for my bed and board in jail.*

"*I never contemplated suicide once while I was in prison, but it's different on the outside.* I have received no counselling or support. Society is treating me like something you'd wipe off the bottom of your shoes, but I'm an innocent man and a victim of a terrible injustice.

"It's horrific. I've been out of jail for 14 months and in that time the state has put me through a war of attrition that it never needed to conduct. I feel my life is disintegrating around me.

"*Making me pay for my bed and board is abhorrent. I was arrested, fitted up and held hostage for 25 years and now they are*

going to charge me for being kept as their prisoner against my will.
 "Can you think of a more disgusting way to abuse someone? I really feel that my heart is truly and finally broken."

2004

THE FREE MARKET

Versailles without War

Many people believe that the Germans deliberately inflated the mark to evade payment of reparations, but that is not true. It was forced on them. This means that the international bankers (such as Bernard Baruch) caused the inflation which eventually brought Hitler to power.

Neutral manufacturers during WWI made enormous fortunes trading with the belligerents, which they then lost speculating in the mark, or extending credit in marks.

In 1914, there were 4 marks to 1 dollar. Even in 1920, despite the war, the mark was a more stable currency than the dollar. During that year, the mark rose from 1 cent to 3 cents, then fell to 1.5 cents, but it was the dollar that was rising – not the mark that was falling.

The German mark was destroyed by the Allies. The Germans offered to pay 40 billion marks in reparations by 1926, but the Allies demanded immediate payment of the costs of occupation without giving the Germans any time in which to raise the money through taxes or borrowing.

This destroyed the value of any reparations received. It destroyed the value of the German taxes which were supposed to pay the reparations. It allowed the Germans to flood the world with goods at absurdly low prices by destroying the foreign exchange value of the mark. It destroyed the value of German war debts owed to foreign countries and expressed in French francs, which rose and fell on the prospect of getting any reparations. It destroyed the value of the pensions owed to French war veterans, which were supposed to be paid out of reparations.

At the same time, the bankers raised interest rates in Britain to 7% and threw 3 million people out of work for 2 years, causing a depression in Britain.

So they destroyed the mark, the franc, British industry, and reparations, all at the same time.

Now, at first glance this seems utterly self-defeating. What did they fight the war for? The Allies kept up the blockade for 9 months after the Armistice, starving hundreds of thousands of Germans to death after the war to force signature of the Versailles Treaty, which was in violation of international law as a violation of the terms of the

Armistice (an academic point, since the Allies also had the right to denounce the Armistice and start fighting again, which they threatened to do – in this sense Hitler was absolutely right in calling Versailles "the greatest breach of faith of all time"). Then they destroyed the value of all the money that they demanded in reparations payments. They destroyed the pensions of the French soldiers who fought in the war, and all competition to German trade abroad. What would be the point of that? (Source: *1922 Encyclopaedia Britannica*, "Speculation", "Currency", "Peace Treaty", etc.)

But on second thought: It's very obvious who profited: international bankers and speculators. The bankers got rich off the war, then they needed an opportunity to reinvest their war profits. So they drove the prices down in Britain and Germany. They weren't manufacturers; they didn't care about bankruptcies. On the contrary: they wanted to buy up bankrupt companies. They didn't care about pension allowances and separation allowances for French soldiers. Why should they?

It might be noted that German industrialists didn't suffer much from the inflation; they extended credits to each other in gold marks (on paper) and promised to pay each other when the mark stabilized. The workers suffered.

These policies are being continued today, and are called "the Free Market". It is asset stripping on a world scale.

1991

THE MASTER PLAN

Machiavelli said that the Prince will retain the outer form of traditional institutions, while changing their inner substance.

The Clinton Revolution, with its Jewish occupation government of Jews, feminists, lesbians, homosexuals, and Negroes (a minority within a minority) show how this is done. It also shows how America could be turned into a Nazi state.

The trick is to run a totally disgusting candidate, in a three-way race, against 2 or 3 other totally disgusting candidates, all of whom are so totally disgusting that no one wants to vote for anyone, but our candidate is a secret "Nazi".

Since all candidates are equally disgusting, but our candidate is marginally less disgusting, or a marginally better liar, than the others, our candidate gets elected. Since he was elected fair and square, with a minimum of cheating, or less cheating than the other candidates, this gives him the right to cram his policies down the country's throat, absolutely regardless of what they are, and no matter how few people want them, even if he breaks every single campaign promise.

If that's not "Democracy", what is? Since when has lying been a bar to holding public office in a "Democracy"?

Now. The first step is to fill all public offices with "Nazis". First to be appointed will be Chairman of the Federal Reserve Board, to get the inside dope on interest rates.

First, we speculate that stock, bond and land prices will fall, then we raise interest rates and shrink the money supply, causing a depression, blaming everything on the policies of the past administration, the "Haters".

Then, at the bottom of the crash (and we will decide where the bottom is), using credit backed by our Federal Reserve notes (which do not cost us anything to print – on the contrary, we will print them for nothing and loan them to the government at 3 or 4 % interest, an infinite return on our investment), we purchase a controlling interest in the American communications media, particularly television, newspapers, magazines, book distribution.

Then we speculate that stock, bond and land prices will rise, and lower interest rates and expand the money supply, causing a boom. Of course, this must be done gradually, because we need a buyer for every seller, but that can be arranged through propaganda. For example, we tell them that the future lies in electronics stocks when the prices are already far too high and we are already selling; that sort of thing.

We now have a stranglehold on the American mind that can never be broken. Just as Americans do not walk because they have cars, they do not think or feel, because they have television.

Of course, under our administration, there will be a slight change in emphasis. "Holocaust Survivor is Tormented by Neo-Nazi Thugs in a Berlin Suburb" will become "Survivor of Allied Terror Bombings Meets the Jewish Financial Criminals Who Caused the War", or, possibly, "Survivor of Mass Rapes in the Congo is Tormented by African Immigrants in a Brussels Suburb". "Brilliantly Intellectual Racially Mixed/Gay/Negro Couple Ridicule Bigoted White Neighbours" will become "Racially Aware White Couple Ridicule Self-Hating Liberals and Race-Traitors", etc.

There will be no censorship. Writers whose material does not meet our standards will not be successful and will starve. That is the free market!

Americans do not understand freedom, and do not believe in it. They are totalitarians with democratic principles. This is all quite natural since they live under a dictatorship themselves, a dictatorship of the Supreme Court. I defy the advocates of democracy to point to one single major change in American public life – the legalization and acceptance of homosexuality, integration, abortion, pornography, near-total non-white immigration, miscegenation, sky-high crime rates, etc. – that was ever decided by anyone's "vote". They are all the result of Supreme Court decisions.

Under the dictatorial power arrogated to itself under John Marshall, America is what the Supreme Court says it will be, no more, and no less. Supreme Court Justices are appointed for life, and they hear only those cases they want to hear. They rule any way they want to rule, and are accountable to no one. If the Supreme Court decided tomorrow that hereditary monarchy and slavery were constitutional, they would be. If the Supreme Court decided tomorrow that cannibal barbecues on the White House lawn were constitutional, they would be. These decisions would be implemented by Federal agents with ruthless and often gratuitous violence, even in the face of bitter opposition of the entire American people.

Laws the Court approves of (exclusively non-white immigration, etc.) are allowed to stand, while laws they do not like (segregation, even if totally voluntary), are declared "unconstitutional".

So, the real key to power in America lies in the Supreme Court. Naturally, Supreme Court justices are all lawyers, and what is more, half of them are Jews. They will do anything for money. So we make them an offer they cannot refuse. We increase their pension benefits. Presto! Nine Jew-lesbian Affirmative Action Negro judges appointed by our horseshit "Democratic" American Presidents take early retirement (followed by a quick swim to Israel), and we appoint nine "Nazis".

It is now discovered that slavery is constitutional, since it was constitutional when the Constitution was written. Segregation (universally practised by our slave-holding Founding Fathers) is also constitutional. All laws to the contrary are null and void. Fortunately, the services of the Negro are no longer required.

Hitler's National Socialist system from 1933 to 1945 was the most popular government in history, and had very little need to use terror tactics against anyone. American imitators will not be so lucky.

Fortunately, a ready-made Federal Gestapo of arsonists, hit-men, and goons are just itching to give all our enemies the "Waco Texas Treatment". Federal agents are all mercenaries, and will always serve the highest bidder. You don't believe it? Just wait.

Americans are cruel, stupid, self-righteous people. Inflamed by television propaganda (formerly a monopoly of the Jews), they commit mass atrocities in a frenzy of religious righteousness. The slightest hint that they have done anything wrong is met with screams of indignation.

The shoe is on the other foot now. America is swept with an iron broom...

1996

UPON BEING CONVICTED OF "INCITEMENT TO RACIAL HATRED"

I just got five months for "incitement to racial hatred". (No details, please; I'm saving them for the *New York Times*.)

Actually, I'm in favour of "hate" laws; I think we need them; I think they are essential. The only problem is, the penalties are nowhere near severe enough!

Is a real criminal impressed by a few months in a reasonably comfortable jail? Of course not. The attitude of a real criminal is, "I've robbed three banks and they're charging me with car theft? What a joke." That's my attitude.

It therefore follows that if we are serious about stamping out "hatred", all forms of "hatred" must be punishable, not by imprisonment, but by more or less instant death by hanging, exactly as at Nuremberg. But I think the procedures and criteria employed should be the same as under the obscenity laws.

For example, back in the good old days (i.e., when we were prosecuting Jews for violating the obscenity laws instead of engineers, chemists, and historians for writing obscure scientific papers about ferric-ferrocyanide compounds in brickwork at Auschwitz), federal, state, and local statutes were often extremely explicit and detailed as to exactly what was prohibited and what was not. There were long lists describing in great detail what was permissible and what was not. (The strictest statutes, surprisingly, were the state laws of Oregon and the city ordinances of Sacramento.)

Nudity, for example, might be entirely acceptable, but there was to be no "*touching*", no "*display of the genitals*", etc., "*in a primarily sexual context*", no "*sexual acts*", whether "*normal or abnormal*", involving "*one or more persons*" of "*the same or opposite sex*", etc. etc. [For example, from the Oregon statute: "*human masturbation, sexual intercourse, or any touching of the genitals, pubic areas or buttocks of the human male or female, or the breasts of the female, whether alone or between members of the same or opposite sex or between humans and animals in an act of apparent sexual stimulation or gratification.*"]

All this broke down under endless hair-splitting by the Jews, who always claim to be unable to understand plain, simple language whenever it suits them.

"*What is art*", what is "*normal*", what constitutes "*redeeming social value*", what is "*patently offensive to the standards of the community*"?, they asked.

What is the "*community*"?, they asked. Is it California, San Francisco, or just North Beach? Does the "*community*" include children? How can you say that deviant pornography is "*offensive*" if it doesn't "*offend*" deviants? Swan Lake in the nude would still be Swan Lake, and that's art; so why isn't cunnilingus on a juke box art, too?

Thousands of court cases later, it was finally decided that "*obscenity*" meant "*appeal to prurient interest*". So in every obscenity trial, the defence lawyer simply asked the prosecution witnesses whether the material appealed to his/her "prurient interest". The question always went something like this:

"*How do you feel about this material personally, do you find it stimulating?*" (Remember, these are prosecution witnesses being asked the question, the people who brought the complaint.) The answer was always,

"*No, I think it's disgusting*", or, "*I think it's boring*". Then, since nobody would ever admit that the stuff turned him/her on, it was argued that it didn't appeal to anybody's "prurient interest", and was therefore not obscene!

In one Supreme Court case (U.S. v. Cohen) [403 U.S. 15 (1971)], it was held that the words "Fuck the Draft" did not appeal to anybody's "prurient interest" and were therefore not obscene; a long series of other cases then held that expressions such as "mother-fucking racist pig cop" did not appeal to anybody's "*prurient interest*" either, so nothing was ever obscene, so everything had to be legalized! [see, for example, Gooding v. Wilson, 405 U.S. 518 (1972); Rosenfeld v. New Jersey, 408 U.S. 901 (1972); Lewis v. City of New Orleans, 408 U.S. 913 (1972); Brown v. Oklahoma, 408 U.S. 914 1972)].

So I say: Do the liberals admit to "hating" anybody because of "racist" epithets (like "nigger", "kike", "gook", "queer", etc.) or "racist" or "Hoaxoco$t-Denial" literature? Of course not. The liberals always claim they're afraid that somebody ELSE might hate somebody! Golly!

OK. Since nobody ever admits to "hating" anybody because of OUR literature, it follows that OUR literature does not constitute the crime of "incitement to racial hatred", and that we cannot be convicted of "hate crimes".

But, since EVERYBODY admits to hating "Nazis" and "racists" because of literature published by Jews, it follows that, while

129

WE cannot be convicted of the crime of "incitement to racial hatred", the Jews CAN be.

Now. Since "hatred" is to be punishable by instant death, this gives us an excuse to clean up America without being accused of "racism" and "anti-Semitism".

Blacks and Mexicans all hate each other, and both hate us (as they will readily admit), so they're all punishable by death; the Chinese, Japanese, Koreans, Cambodians, Vietnamese, etc. all hate each other, so it's in the "drinko" with "El Chinko", etc. etc.

Homosexuals, by way of variety (since they like variety so much), will be convicted of "heterophobic hysteria" and will be exiled to one of our Pleasure Island FAGULAGS (faggot gulags) in the frozen tundra of the North, where they will be allowed to do what they like to each other, but will be denied police protection and medical care.

When they get done robbing, murdering, and torturing each other, and infecting each other with all their filthy diseases, that will be the end of this year's faggot crop (until next year – presumably, in a sane society, each year's crop would be somewhat smaller). To keep them "stoned" in accordance with Biblical teachings, we'll air-drop them poppers and alcohol on Sunday morning – but no food, unless they can grow it. *Homo, homo, on the range-o, R.I.P.*

Presto! An all-white Christian America. No more niggers; no more gooks; no more coons, kikes, queers, and spooks. And all without racism, anti-Semitism, RICO, or even the conspiracy laws (which we can still use, of course) – just good, old-fashioned, "hate" laws.

The Jews think they can always twist everything just to suit themselves. Well, we'll just have to twist things right back again. Twisting words always ends with twisting necks.

FINIS.

[All legal references are from chapter 54, "*Defense of an Obscenity Case*", by Richard I. Targow and Paul N. Savoy, in *Criminal Defense Techniques*, The Matthew Bender Co., edited by Sidney Bernstein, 1984 update.]

1996

IN MEMORIAM – A DEDICATION

R.I.P.

Aimee Willard, murder victim, obviously of Irish or Scottish ancestry.

Her killer, a parole violator with a prior murder conviction, says he is being "framed because he is black".

How many black criminals is this one young life worth? 100? 1,000? A million? Ten billion?

When I look into the eyes of this beautiful, smiling, dead young girl, I feel that no sacrifice is too great if it helps save even one young life like this. At any rate, a great deal more than just one young life is at stake.

Carlos W. Porter
20 November 2005

"Life springs from death, and from the graves of patriot men and women spring living nations."

– Pádraig Pearse, shot 3 May 1916

www.ingramcontent.com/pod-product-compliance
Lightning Source LLC
LaVergne TN
LVHW091556060526
838200LV00036B/868